新东方
NEW ORIENTAL

MW01686981

雅思口语

IELTS

SPEAKING

新东方雅思考试指定辅导教程——基础培训

新东方教育科技集团雅思研究院 著

西安交通大学出版社
XI'AN JIAOTONG UNIVERSITY PRESS

图书在版编目(CIP)数据

雅思口语/新东方教育科技集团雅思研究院著. —西安：西安交通大学出版社，2009（2012.11 重印）

ISBN 978-7-5605-3118-2

Ⅰ. 雅… Ⅱ. 新… Ⅲ. 英语—口语—高等教育—自学参考资料 Ⅳ. H319.9

中国版本图书馆 CIP 数据核字(2009) 第 059032 号

Acknowledgements

This publication was designed by Madelize Bekker and Dorothy Cleary.

We would also like to thank the following authors for their contributions:

Sarah Balfour

Pauline Newell

Chris Orange

Sheryl Read

Jane Wilson

The Curriculum Factory Team

书 名	雅思口语
著 者	新东方教育科技集团雅思研究院
责任编辑	董云梅
封面设计	赵文康
出版发行	西安交通大学出版社
地 址	西安市兴庆南路 10 号(邮编:710049)
电 话	(010)62605588 62605019(发行部) (029)82668315(总编室)
读者信箱	bj62605588@163.com
印 刷	北京画中画印刷有限公司
字 数	299 千
开 本	889mm×1194mm 1/16
印 张	12.75
版 次	2012 年 11 月第 1 版第 12 次印刷
书 号	ISBN 978-7-5605-3118-2/H·915
定 价	48.00 元

Dear Student,

Welcome to this New Oriental IELTS preparation course and the Speaking Book in particular.

IELTS, the International English Language Testing System, is one of the world's most popular English language tests for entry into university or higher education where English is the language of communication.

The Speaking Test, although relatively short (11-14 minutes), is often the most nerve-wracking module in IELTS because you are face to face with the examiner. Not only that, but you have to listen, process the examiner's language, and answer the question clearly, using correct grammatical structures and with only a minimum of hesitation.

This book is designed to help you prepare for all these elements of the test in a systematic way. Firstly, you will learn a lot of useful words for dealing with familiar and abstract topics and you will be encouraged to expand your vocabulary. Having a wide range of vocabulary will give you confidence in the test.

You will also find extensive pronunciation exercises to help you with some of the more problematic sounds of English. The grammar exercises have been chosen specifically so that you are able to answer familiar questions using the appropriate tenses and talk about unfamiliar, more abstract issues using the appropriate functions (for example, opinion, comparison, contrast, analysing, speculation).

This book will guide you through the best approaches to all three parts of the IELTS Speaking test using the most typical topics with opportunities for extensive practice and consolidation.

Congratulations on choosing to study IELTS with New Oriental.

Ready? Let's go!

Rod Ellis

第二语言教学之父
"Task Base" 教学法创始人

Preface

Dear Student,

Thank you for choosing to study for the IELTS with New Oriental.

This book is the long anticipated result of a close cooperation between New Oriental and international IELTS experts to develop our own IELTS training materials. We believe it offers a different approach, with the following features:

First of all, the language used is likely what you will encounter in a real classroom or work setting while living abroad. The setting of each dialogue is also consistent with how you might encounter English as used by native speakers in their own country.

Also, under the guidance of renowned professor Rod Ellis, our partner international research team has delivered a proven methodology for ensuring the intended acquisition of needed skills for IELTS test takers in speaking, listening, reading and writing.

And most importantly, this book incorporates ten years of IELTS training experience by the very best teachers at New Oriental, and therefore has been customized to suit the needs of Chinese students.

I sincerely hope that together with these materials New Oriental teachers can make your IELTS classroom fruitful and rewarding. Enjoy your learning time with New Oriental!

周成刚

新东方教育科技集团

Overview

We hope you will enjoy using this book, and that you will learn useful language and skills to help you to pass the IELTS speaking test. This book covers the following points:

Vocabulary and Common Expressions for IELTS speaking topics—*this matches to 'vocabulary' in the marking criteria for the IELTS speaking test.*
Each unit in this book has a Vocabulary Bank which includes useful words and expressions for discussing the topic.

Pronunciation Exercises—*this matches to 'Pronunciation' in the marking criteria for the IELTS speaking test.*
You will practice:

- Pronouncing individual words
- Linking words together
- Word and sentence stress
- Accurate use of rhythm and intonation for speaking in English

Grammar—*this matches to 'Grammar' in the marking criteria for the IELTS speaking test.*
Useful and common grammar that you will need to successfully speak about the topics in the IELTS speaking test.
For example:

- The most common verb tenses and how and where to use them
- Correct grammar structures for describing things, telling stories about your own experience, comparing past and present events, speculating about the future and giving opinions

Structuring answers and linking ideas together—*this matches to 'Fluency and Coherence' in the marking criteria for the IELTS speaking test.*
For example:

- Useful and common ways to link ideas in speaking
- Ways to begin and extend and answer
- Practice in building fluency and confidence when discussing common IELTS speaking topics

All three parts of the IELTS speaking test are covered and practised in this book.

Work hard, take every opportunity to practice, enjoy your study and succeed in the IELTS Speaking test!

Good luck!

Contents

IELTS

Speaking

"Chance favors the prepared mind."

(Louis Pasteur)

UNIT 1 Education

Focus on Part 1 of the IELTS Speaking Test

WARM-UP

1 *Listen to these sentences and repeat them.*

a. I'm an English student.
b. I'm studying at New Oriental Foreign Language School.
c. I need to improve my English.
d. I want to take the IELTS exam.
e. It's a lot of fun! Or: It's an important language to learn.
f. I come from Beijing.

2 *Now, listen and repeat these questions.*

a. What's your first name?
b. What's your family name?
c. Where do you come from?
d. Are you a student or do you have a job?
e. Why are you studying English?
f. Where are you studying English?
g. What do you enjoy about studying English?

3 *Work with a partner. Ask and answer the questions above.*

VOCABULARY

4 *Check the meaning of the following words in your dictionary.*

Vocabulary Bank

subject	public	sports	rules
class	discipline	library	uniform
physics	homework	language	gymnasium
chemistry	assignments	history	laboratory
maths	test	culture	absent
compulsory	marks	strict	attendance
optional	exams	hit	junior
co-ed	primary	corporal	senior
single sex	secondary	punishment	science
private	naughty	detention	major

5 *Look at the questions below and decide which words above could be used to answer these questions. Some words could be used for many questions. The first one has been done for you.*

Let's talk about education:

For example:

a. What subjects are compulsory in your school?
   Answer: Maths / language / history
b. What are your favourite subjects?
c. What subjects do you not like?
d. Tell me about discipline in your school.
e. What exams do you take?
f. How much homework do you have?

6 *Listen to the words in the Vocabulary Bank and repeat them.*

7 *Some words have one sound or syllable and some have two or more. Write the words from the Vocabulary Bank in the correct column below.*

1 syllable	2 syllables	3 or more syllables
hit	public	optional

PRONUNCIATION

Sentence stress. In English, words that carry the main meaning, i.e. important words, are stressed, i.e. they are said louder or stronger.

8 *Listen to the audio and underline the stressed words in each sentence below. The first one has been done for you.*

a. What subjects are compulsory in your school?
In my school we have to take language and maths but we can choose history or chemistry.

b. What are your favourite subjects?
I really like English because it's so interesting and the teacher is so funny!

c. What subjects do you not like?
I hate maths because it's boring and it's too hard.

d. Tell me about discipline in your school.
Our school is very strict. There are lots of rules. You have to wear a uniform and you can't talk in class.

e. What exams do you take?
At the end of Senior High everyone takes the University Entrance exam. It's really difficult and we have to do a lot of work.

f. How much homework do you have?
Lots! I have to work every night and I get so tired!

GRAMMAR

Like / love / hate / don't like +V-ing

9 *Think about your typical school day and all the activities and things you have to do. Make a list with your partner.*

A school day in the life of ...			
a.	*maths lesson with Mr. Brown*	*f.*	....
b.	....	*g.*	....
c.	....	*h.*	....
d.	....	*i.*	....
e.	....	*j.*	....

Words to express liking or not liking:

hate — *don't like/dislike* — *don't mind* — *like* — *really like* — *love*

10 Work by yourself and write activities from your school day into the boxes below to show how you feel about doing these activities.

Hate	Don't Like /Dislike	Don't mind	Like	Really like	Love
					e.g. maths lesson

When expressing how you feel about doing activities, you can use the following language:

hate, like, don't mind, love +v-ing

I love studying maths

I like/don't like learning English

I don't mind doing chemistry

I hate studying history

In English we don't say: I ~~very~~ like studying…

We say: I really like studying…

TIP

Remember that it is good to give a little extra information like a reason or an example when you answer a question or talk about a topic.

How do you feel about the activities you do at school each day?

I love studying maths because I have a great teacher.

I really like learning history because it's so interesting, for example, the Ming dynasty.

11 With your partner, tell how you feel about the activities you do during your school day. Give a reason or an example for each activity.

Error correction

Find the mistakes in the following speaking excerpts. Write the correct sentence in the space below. The first one has been done for you.

a. I ~~am~~ come from a small town in Hunan Province, China.
<u>I come from a small town in Hunan Province, China.</u>

b. I don't like learn history because it is not useful to me. helpful

____

c. I not like studying biology as it is so difficult for me to understand science.

____

d. I like study English because it's an important language to learn.

____

e. I very like studying maths because I want to be a maths teacher.

____

Put it all together

12 With your partner, ask and answer the following questions about <u>your</u> school. There are some ideas given to help you with the answers.

Questions	Answers
a. What subjects are compulsory in your school?	In my school we have to... but we can choose...
b. What are your favourite subjects?	I really like... because it's... and...
c. What subjects do you dislike?	I dislike... because it's ...
d. Tell me about the discipline in your school.	Our school is... You have to...
e. What exams do you take?	At the end of...
f. How much homework do you have?	Lots! I have to...

Focus on Part 2 of the IELTS Speaking Test

In Part 2 of the IELTS Speaking test, the candidate has to speak for 1-2 minutes on a topic that the examiner gives. This is called 'the long turn'.

The examiner will give you a prompt card and tell you that you have one minute to read the card and prepare your answer. The examiner will give you a piece of paper and a pencil to make notes. You should write only short notes. Long sentences are not possible as there is only one minute to prepare.

13 Read the following Part Two prompt card:

Describe a teacher you remember well.
You should say:
what the teacher was like
which subject(s) he or she taught
what you enjoyed about his or her classes
and explain why you remember this teacher in particular.

14 Now listen to a student talking about this topic and answer the following questions:

a. Did the student like the teacher?
b. Why?

TIP
The speaker has used lots of examples to expand her answer. This makes it easier to fill the one to two minutes required for the long turn in Part 2.

FLUENCY AND COHERENCE

15 Read the Part 2 answer below and write short notes in the boxes on the right about the three different parts of the talk.

***Only** write main important words in your short notes, e.g. nouns, adjectives and verbs. The first one has been done for you.*

Structure of the Talk:	Short Notes:
§1: What the teacher was like (personality and appearance)	Wonderful, friendly, kind Strict—strap,short,loud voice Mrs T
§2: What subjects she taught	
§3: What the speaker enjoyed about her classes	
§4: Why the speaker remembered her	

Part 2 Answer:

§ 'I remember a teacher I had at primary school who was wonderful. From the first day she was friendly and kind towards the students, who were eight years old. But she was also strict. I mean, on the first day, she took out this old fashioned strap and banged it on the desk and we all got such a fright, but she was just trying to show us she was in control. She wasn't really that scary although she was quite short and she spoke in a loud voice. Everybody called her Mrs T.'

§ 'She taught us for every subject, so she taught us English, maths, writing, and actually I can't remember what else! '

§ 'I guess what I used to enjoy most about her classes was her personality and the fact that she cared about all of her students, even the naughty ones. I remember her daughter lived in America and she used to send over American sweets and chewing gum for Mrs T to give to the good students. All the students tried to be really good to get that reward! '

§ 'I particularly remember my teacher, Mrs T, because she was so kind, helpful and patient. I was very young and she was like a mother to me, gentle but strict at the same time.'

Note the structure the speaker uses to talk about a past habit that no longer happens:

used to + base verb.

I used to enjoy…
She used to send over American sweets…

For example:

'I used to go the library.'—a past habit. This was something I did often in the past, but I don't do it any more.
'I used to live in Shanghai.'—a past state. I don't live there any more.

16 Read the examples below and answer the questions.

a. I **used to smoke** cigarettes. Do I smoke cigarettes now? __________

b. I **didn't use to speak** English. Do I speak English now? __________

c. **I used to** live in Australia. Do I live in Australia now? __________

17 Now write some examples of what you used to do when you were young.

Remember they must be past habits or states.

a. ______________________________

b. ______________________________

c. ______________________________

d. ______________________________

e. ______________________________

One of the best ways to become more fluent in English is to practise doing 'long turns'. Here are some practices for you.

18 Take some time to prepare short notes on the following topic:

Describe your first school.
You should say:
the name of the school and where it was
activities you liked at school
activities you didn't like
and whether it was a good school or not.

	Your Short Notes:
Name of school, location	
Activities you liked and why	
Activities you didn't like and why	
A good school? Why / why not?	

19 With a partner, take turns to speak for at least half a minute. Remember to use examples and give reasons. If you have a watch, time each other.

UNIT 2 Food

Focus on Part 1 of the IELTS Speaking Test

WARM-UP

1 *Look at the following types of food. Decide if each type of food is healthy or junk food and write the words in the table below.*

hamburger	apple	rice	banana	tomato
noodles	fried chicken	hotdog	chicken	bread
biscuits	cake	cabbage	chips	cheeseburger
pizza	dumpling	ice cream	chocolate	egg
salad	potato	lettuce	sandwich	celery
cheese	pasta	spinach	sushi	meat pie

Healthy Food	Junk Food
e.g. apple	hamburger

2 *Listen and mark the stressed syllable on each word.*

VOCABULARY

Vocabulary Bank

Food (nouns)	Food can be...	Food can taste...	Good / bad food is...
barbecue	burnt	bitter	appetizing
brunch	dry	bland	delicious
cake	fatty	salty	disgusting
fruit	fresh	savoury	junk
meal	greasy	sour	revolting
pasta	healthy	spicy	tasty
picnic	mouldy	sweet	vile
pizza	raw		yucky (acceptable slang)
restaurant	rich		yummy (acceptable slang)
snack	stale		
steak	succulent		
supper	undercooked		
vegetables	wholesome		

Food can be ... (how it's cooked)
baked
barbecued
boiled
(deep) fried
grilled
microwaved
roasted
steamed
stewed
stir-fried
toasted

3 Listen to some students answering Part 1 IELTS speaking questions.

- **Speaker 1:** My family and I always do our food shopping at the local markets because all the fruit and vegetables are so fresh.
- **Speaker 2:** I really like fast food, and my favourite is pizza — yummy!
- **Speaker 3:** I never cook because I don't know how! My parents always cook for me.
- **Speaker 4:** I prefer eating in restaurants to eating at home, because you don't have to do the dishes afterwards!
- **Speaker 5:** We usually eat toast or cereal with fruit for breakfast and on the weekend we might go out for bacon and eggs.

4 Now listen and repeat these sentences from the previous activity.

a. I never cook because I don't know how.
b. I really like fast food.
c. I prefer eating in restaurants to eating at home.
d. My favourite food is pizza.
e. We usually eat toast or cereal for breakfast.

5 Match the questions below with the answers above.

i. What's your favourite food? ⟶ d. My favourite food is pizza.
ii. Do you like to cook?
iii. Do you prefer to eat out or eat at home?
iv. What do you usually eat for breakfast?
v. Do you like fast food?

6 Listen and you will notice the important words in each example below are stressed: they are said louder and stronger than the other words. Underline the stressed words in each question. The first one has been done for you.

a. Tell me about your **<u>favourite</u>** food.
b. Do you like to cook?
c. Do you prefer to eat out or eat at home?
d. What do you usually eat for breakfast?
e. Do you like fast food?

7 Listen again and repeat the sentences using the same stress pattern as in the audio.

8 Now work with a partner to ask and answer the questions using your own words. Remember to stress the important words.

I love all Chinese food, but my favourite is probably noodle soup, because it has so many flavours.

a. What is your favourite food?

b. Do you like to cook?
c. Do you prefer to eat out or eat at home?
d. What do you usually eat for breakfast?
e. Do you like fast food?

PRONUNCIATION

9 *Circle as many 'food' words as you can find in the two lines below.*

Souphotdogtastepizzahutdonutsweetsnackoverweightsoftdrinkchocolatebigmaccarrotbreakfastchipchicke
nnuggetdietfastmilkweighteat

10 *Listen to check and put the words in the right category.*

/p/ ending	/t/ ending	/k/ ending
Soup		

11 *Listen again and repeat the words.*

12 *Now listen to the following sentences and repeat.*

a. A soft drink is unhealthy because it contains a lot of sugar.
b. Pizza Hut is a worldwide fast food restaurant.
c. If you want to lose weight, you shouldn't eat too much junk food.
d. A balanced diet is an important part of keeping healthy.
e. He eats a hotdog every day.
f. Chocolate milk is very tasty.
g. People often eat dumplings for breakfast in China.
h. I eat a carrot every day as part of a healthy diet.

i. Bananas are the perfect fruit.
j. He ate too many Big Macs and now he is overweight.

Often in English, the last letter of one word joins onto the next word. Listen to the following sentence: Chocolate milk is very tasty.
It sounds like: Chocolate <u>mil kis</u> very tasty.

This is because the final 'k' sound of milk joins with the vowel 'i' in is. This is a common feature of spoken English. If one word ends in a consonant and the next word begins with a vowel, the consonant links onto the vowel of the next word.

13 Listen to the following sentences and mark the linking sounds.

a. Soft drinks are not very healthy.
b. Pizza Hut is a fast food restaurant.
c. It's important to eat healthy food.
d. He likes to eat a hotdog for lunch.

14 Listen again and repeat the sentences making sure you link words correctly.

15 Now say the sentences again to your partner.

Sometimes, you will need to ask the examiner to repeat the question. Here is some useful language to do this:

Your intonation is important. When using these phrases, your voice should go up at the end of the word or sentence. In English, this shows politeness. For example:

Pardon?

16 Listen and repeat the phrases after you hear them.

17 Work in pairs. Use the questions below to practise the language above. One person asks a question and the other asks for repetition using one of the examples above. Focus on using the correct intonation and make sure you practise with all of the examples.

- What's your favourite food?
- Do you like to cook?
- Do you prefer to eat out or eat at home?
- What do you usually eat for breakfast?
- Do you like fast food?

Sorry, I didn't hear you. Could you repeat the question?

GRAMMAR

18 Look at the following answer from the previous activity:

I prefer eating in restaurants to eating at home.

Prefer is a verb which means you like something better than something else.

I prefer Chinese food to McDonalds.

When you are expressing preferences, you can also compare one thing to another.

I like hamburgers more than rice.

I don't like McDonalds as much as KFC.

19 Look at the food in the table below. Which do you prefer for each option? Write your answer in the 'your preference' column. The first one has been done for you.

Option 1:	Option 2:	Your preference
1. Hamburgers	Dumplings	Hamburgers
2. Chocolate	Rice	
3. KFC	Pizza Hut	
4. Coca cola	Pepsi	
5. Donuts	Bananas	
6. Spinach	Cheeseburgers	
7. Sprite	Green tea	
8. Subway	McDonalds	

20 Write sentences about which foods you prefer using the 'preference language' given in the box above.

For example:

I prefer dumplings to hamburgers.

OR I like dumplings more than hamburgers.
OR I don't like hamburgers as much as dumplings.

21 *Now tell someone else about your preferences.*

22 *You can also use a comparative adjective to give a reason for your preference.*

What do you prefer, hamburgers or dumplings?

I prefer dumplings to hamburgers, because they are healthier.

Comparative Language	
Short Adjectives	Hot—hotter—hottest
Adjectives ending in -y	Hungry—hungrier—hungriest (change the -y to an -i)
Adjectives with 3 syllables or more	Important—more important—most important

23 *Write the comparative forms of each adjective below. Check any words you don't know in your dictionary.*

a. healthy ________ +
b. tasty ________
c. sweet ________
d. oily ________
e. greasy ________
f. spicy ________
g. delicious ________
h. yummy ________

24 *Now decide whether the adjectives have a positive or negative meaning. Put a plus sign [+] next to the positive ones and a minus sign [-] next to the negative ones. The first one has been done for you.*

25 *Work with a partner and ask them which food they prefer. Use a comparative adjective (e.g. healthier) in your answer.*

For example:

I prefer dumplings because they are healthier.
I prefer apples because they are sweeter.

Put it all together

26 Fill in the gaps with your own answers.

1. Do you like to try food from other cultures?	I like to try____________food because it is ____________.
2. Do you prefer to cook for yourself or have other people cook for you?	I prefer to____________________because ____________________.
3. Which do you prefer: fast food or healthy food?	I prefer____________________as it is ________________.
4. Is there any food you would like to try but haven't?	I haven't tried______________,but I would really like to. I think it would be ____________.
5. Which is your favourite fast food restaurant?	My favourite fast food restaurant is probably ____________, which serves ________food, such as____________.
6. What do you usually eat for lunch?	I eat____________,and ____________,for lunch.
7. Do you prefer to eat at a fast food restaurant with your family or with your friends?	I prefer to eat with my______________at a restaurant as I like to____________.
8. Which kind of fast food do you like least?	I really don't like_______________because ________________________.
9. What type of fast food do you like?	I like______________________because ______________.
10. Where do you normally buy food?	I usually buy food at_________________or ______________________.
11. Do you prefer sweet food or savoury food?	I enjoy________more than______________. I love_____________!

27 Work with a partner to ask and answer the questions.

Focus on Part 2 of the IELTS Speaking Test

Describe a meal you particularly enjoyed.
You should mention:
where you ate
what you ate
who you were with
and and why you enjoyed it.

28 *Listen to a student speaking about this topic.*

'I'm going to talk about a meal I enjoyed. It was right after my university graduation, when I was about 21. My whole family came to see me graduate and it was a very proud day. After the ceremony we all went to a nearby restaurant, which was busy with other families who were all doing the same thing. The atmosphere was exciting and busy. The restaurant was beautiful, with long tables, candles and flowers. My family also gave me a huge bunch of flowers and some cards and special gifts. I was there with my mum, dad, two brothers and my grandfather and I remember that we ordered a lot of seafood and champagne to celebrate. I can't really remember what else we ate, but the seafood was delicious. Oh, that's right, we had lobster to share, which was amazing. We spent all afternoon at the restaurant, talking, eating and laughing. And of course, we took lots of photos. My father made a speech of congratulations and wished me good luck for the future. It was such an enjoyable day because I knew that my family was very proud of me and we all shared my celebration together. And everything about the restaurant was perfect. The waiters were friendly and the food was fantastic. I am happy that I remember this special day in my life so clearly.'

29 *Answer the following questions:*

a. What did the student eat?
b. Why was the meal special?

30 *Look at the script. Circle the present tense verbs and underline the past simple verbs. What do you notice about the tenses the speaker has mainly used?*

FLUENCY AND COHERENCE

31 *Think about a meal you have enjoyed and make your own answer to the prompt card. Use these questions to help you make notes before you speak.*

Question	Your notes
• Where did you eat? Was it a restaurant/your home/friend's house/party/picnic/family member's house? Describe.	
• What did you eat? Describe in detail.	
• Who were you with? Family/friends/classmates/boy-friend/girl-friend/acquaintance?	
• Describe the waiters.	
• Why did you enjoy it? Was it a special occasion or celebration (birthday/wedding/graduation etc.)? Was it special because of the people you were with? Or the food?	
• Did anything funny, interesting or unusual happen?	

32 *Now use your notes to talk to your partner for one minute on this topic.*

33 *After making brief notes on each of the following topics, choose one to talk about.*

- What you ate for breakfast today.
- Your favourite fast food restaurant.
- A type of food you love.

UNIT 3 Sport and Exercise

Focus on Part 1 of the IELTS Speaking Test

WARM-UP

1 *Listen and repeat the sentences below.*

a. I play basketball with my friends every day after school.
b. I'm not very good at soccer, but I love it.
c. In my free time, I often like watching tennis matches on television.
d. I don't watch rugby very much because it's not very popular in China.
e. On the weekends, I play table tennis with my dad.

VOCABULARY

2 *Look at the following sports. Can you add any more to the list?*

hockey soccer rugby athletics gymnastics volleyball table tennis swimming golf American football basketball cycling skiing snowboarding skating kayaking tennis weightlifting squash surfing boxing motor racing badminton show jumping snooker sailing

3 *Classify the sports into the following four categories:*

I like to play/go	*I like to watch*	*I am not interested in ... at all*	*I would like to try*

There are usually three verbs which go together with various sports:

play, go and do

For example:

I **go** surfing (only used with + v-ing)
He **plays** basketball (sports with no -ing ending)

We use the verb **do** with the following sports: athletics, gymnastics.

TIP

'play' is often associated with a sport that uses a ball
'go' often means there is no set area in which the sportsperson has to move (freedom to move anywhere)
'do' has the sense of confinement. e.g. a stage, a ring, an arena

4 *Match the sports from Activity 2 with the appropriate verb.*

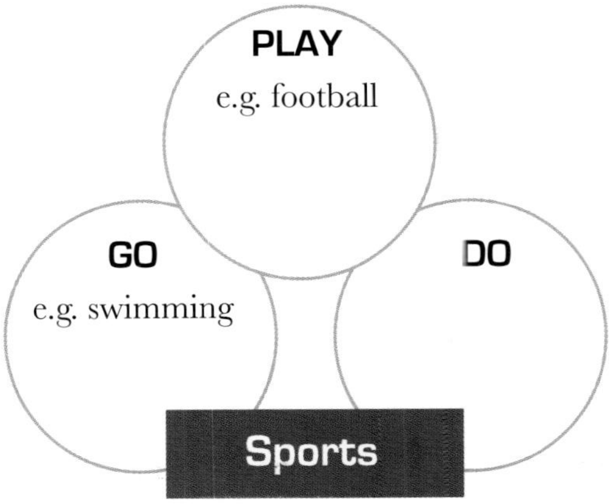

5 *Write five sentences about yourself using the vocabulary you have learned so far.*

6 *Say your sentences to a partner.*

7 *Make questions for your partner using the prompts below. The first one has been done as an example.*

a. Do you prefer to exercise alone or with friends?
(prefer/exercise alone/or with friends)

b. ______________________________
(like/go/swimming in the sea)

c. ______________________________
(how/often/go/running)

d. ______________________________
(exercise/regularly)

e. ______________________________
(think/exercise/important)

8 Listen to the model and check your answers.

9 Listen again and repeat each question.

fun　good for me　relaxing
competitive　keeps me fit
interesting　helps me relax

10 Ask and answer the questions with your partner. Use an adjective or phrase from the words above to help you give a reason for your answer.

Do you prefer to exercise alone or with friends?

Probably with friends because it is more fun!

Vocabulary Bank

Types of sporting events	Places & people associated with sporting events	Sporting events can be ...	Actions that take place during sporting events
challenge	arena	dangerous	attack
championship	challenger	dramatic	bowl
competition	coach	dynamic	catch
final	court	exhilarating	chase
friendly match	gymnasium	memorable	defend
semi-final	opponent	nail-biting	dodge
tournament	opposition	nerve-racking	intercept
	referee	tense	jump
	reserve	thrilling	kick
	ring	tough	pass
	stadium	uneventful	save
	supporter		score
	umpire		sprint
			tackle
			throw

11 *Choose five sports and brainstorm the equipment you need to play them. Also, write the verb you need to talk about these sports:* ***play, go*** *or* ***do****. The first one has been done for you as an example.*

Sport	Equipment	Verb
a. Table tennis (ping pong)	Ping pong table, bats, net and ball	Play
b.		
c.		
d.		
e.		

12 *Use the table above to ask each other questions about the sports.*

For example:

A. Tell me more about ping pong. What equipment do you need for it?
B: Oh, ping pong is a fun game to play. I really like playing ping pong because you don't need a lot of equipment —just a table, bats, net and a ball!

PRONUNCIATION

/v/ and /w/

The /v/ sound is made by resting the top teeth on your bottom lip and using your voice. When you practise pronouncing /v/, bite your bottom lip a little. Try it.
The /w/ sound is made by starting with your lips together in an 'o' shape and then voicing the sound as your lips separate. When you practise pronouncing /w/, pull your lips in hard. Try it.

13 *Now listen to the following words from this unit and decide whether they are /v/ or /w/. Write them in the correct box below.*

/v/	/w/

14 *Listen again and practice saying each word.*

GRAMMAR

Adverbs of Frequency:
These tell us how often things are done. Look at the example below:

A: How often do you go to the movies?
B: Oh, I often go to the movies. Probably once a week, at least.

15 Write the following adverbs of frequency on the continuum below:

often	hardly ever	sometimes		a lot
not very often	not very much	quite often	quite a lot	always

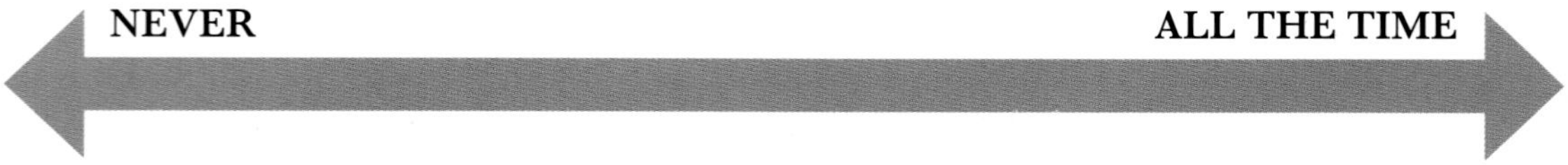

16 Fill in the gaps in the dialogues below using an adverb of frequency. The first one has been done for you.

a. A: Do you go swimming at the pool very often?
B: Yes, quite a lot. It relaxes me.

b. A: Do you watch football on television much?
B: _____! I hate it.

c. A: How often do you go jogging?
B: Well, I try to go ________________, but sometimes I just feel like sleeping instead!

d. A: Do you study English much at home?
B: ______________. I always forget my homework.

TIP
When you are speaking about things you do regularly, you use the present simple tense. For example: 'I watch basketball on television every day. Sometimes, I go to the swimming pool and swim 20 lengths.' I don't play golf very often.

17 Listen to each dialogue and check your answers.

18 Listen again and repeat.

Adverbs of frequency are usually placed in the middle of a sentence between the subject and the verb or at the end of the sentence. However, *a lot* and *quite a lot* are placed after the object, *much* and *very much* are placed at the end of the sentence.	
Positive	I sometimes play tennis at the weekend. I often go swimming with my friends. I play table tennis quite a lot because I like it.
Negative	I don't usually watch sport on television. She doesn't go jogging very much.
Question	Do you often go swimming? Does he play tennis a lot?

19 Insert the adverb of frequency given in brackets into the following sentences in the correct position. The first one has been done for you.

a. I play soccer because I like it. (quite a lot)
   I play soccer quite a lot because I like it.
b. Do you play table tennis? (often)
c. My dad watches soccer on television with me. (sometimes)
d. I don't watch sport on television. (very much)
e. My mum comes to watch my tennis matches. (quite a lot)
f. I go swimming at the pool because I like it. (always)

20 Ask and answer the questions below with your partner. In the answer, talk about your own experience and include adverbs of frequency.

a. Do you go swimming at the pool very often?
b. Do you watch football on television much?
c. How often do you go jogging?
d. Do you exercise in a gym?
e. Do you play tennis?
f. Do you like watching sport on TV?

Focus on Part 2 of the IELTS Speaking Test

FLUENCY AND COHERENCE

PROMPT CARD 1

Talk about a sport that you enjoy playing.
You should say:
  which sport it is
  what equipment is used
  how it is played
and explain why you enjoy playing it.

PROMPT CARD 2

Talk about a sport that you would like to try.
You should say:
  what it is
  what equipment you would need
  how it is played
and explain why you want to try it.

21 Listen to the following two speakers talking about these topics. Decide whether they are speaking about prompt card 1 or prompt card 2.

Speaker 1: Prompt card ________
Speaker 2: Prompt card ________

22 Look at the language from Speaker 1. Use the language to write your own notes about a sport you enjoy playing.

To play..........................you need ....

The aim of the game is to ....
....

Players do this by ....
....

is played...

In my team, I play.....................so I have to ....

I'm also pretty good at ....
....

I guess I like playing .... because...

I feel ....when I play ....

Speaker 1:

Okay, I'm going to speak about a sport that I enjoy playing: basketball. To play basketball, you need a ball, a court, and two hoops at either end. Of course, you also need players—five on each side. The aim of the game is to get the ball through the hoop at each end. Players do this by dribbling the basketball down the court and passing it to other players to move the ball in the right direction. Meanwhile, the members of the other team try to stop them from doing this. They can try to stop them by guarding them very closely and trying to get the ball from them. Basketball is played in four quarters, and players can be swapped during this time. It takes about an hour but that depends on how often the referee stops them. In my team, I play centre and so I have to run around a lot and help move the basketball down the court. I'm also pretty good at shooting, so I get lots of chances to score points. I guess I like playing basketball because of the way it makes me feel. I feel quite excited when I play and it also feels good to be part of a team, especially when we're winning!

23 Look at the language from Speaker 2. Use the language to write your own notes about a sport you would like to try.

A sport that I'd like to try is..

I'm keen to try it because..

You need a lot of equipment: ....

....

You start off..

I'd love to try it because..

Speaker 2

A sport that I'd like to try is white water rafting. I guess it's more of an extreme sport really. I've always been keen to try it, ever since I saw a programme on television which showed people rafting on this huge river in South America somewhere. It looked amazing, but scary at the same time. To do white water rafting, I think you need to go with a company who organises it all for you, because you need a lot of stuff: lifejackets, helmets, wetsuits and all that kind of thing. The boats they use are inflatable rafts, and you are given little paddles to row with. From what I saw, you start off at the top of a river and float down until you get to a type of small waterfall, where the water is moving very fast, and the raft goes over and down to the next part of the river. That's when it gets exciting! I saw people falling out and going under the water, but they all looked like they were having a great time. I'd love to try it because it looks so exciting and a little bit dangerous at the same time, so I think it'd be quite thrilling. And I love swimming, so hopefully I'd be Okay!

24 Work with a partner and practise speaking using your notes to help you. You can choose to talk about prompt card 1 or prompt card 2.

25 When your partner has finished speaking, ask one question about what he or she talked about. In the IELTS Speaking test, the examiner will usually ask one or two follow-up questions after the Part 2 long turn.

UNIT 4 Media

Focus on Part 1 of the IELTS Speaking Test

WARM-UP

1 Work with a partner. Ask each other:

What is your favourite television programme? Why do you like it?

2 There are different types of movies and television programmes. Continue to work with your partner and think of examples of movies or television programmes that match each of the types below. The first one has been done for you.

Types of Movies and Television Programmes			
Sports Soccer World Cup	Comedy	Horror Movie	Romance
Science Fiction	Documentary	Quiz Action	Movie

3 Ask your partner:

Which type of movie or television programme do you prefer? And why?

VOCABULARY

Vocabulary Bank

Types of movies, radio and TV programmes	Describing movies, radio and TV programmes	Collocations
Chat show	Educational	I was terrified
Sports programme	Old fashioned	It was terrifying
Documentary	Modern	I was scared
Music programme	Scary	It was scary
Horror movie	Terrifying	I was amused
Quiz	Interesting	It was amusing
Comedy	Fascinating	It's a true story
Romance	Funny	It's based on fact
Action movie	Amusing	It's partly true
Autobiography	Humorous	It's fiction
Biography	Exciting	It got my attention
Historical movie	Boring	Good looking actor
Fiction	Relaxing	Good looking actress
Science Fiction	Popular	
Martial arts	Famous	
Drama		
Crime		
Cartoon		
Fantasy		
News		
Current affairs		
Weather report		
Musical		
Western		
Thriller		

PRONUNCIATION

4 *Listen to the audio and mark the stressed syllable in each word or phrase in the columns above. Some phrases have two stressed syllables.*

For example:

It's a **true sto**ry.

5 Listen again and repeat making sure you say the stressed syllables louder and longer.

6 Listen to the following chant. Listen again and repeat (on the audio there is a pause after each line.) Make sure your pronunciation is correct.

Funny, funnier, funniest
The funniest show on TV
This *programme's the funniest
The best one for you to see.

Scary, scarier, scariest
The scariest show on TV
This *programme's the scariest
The worst one for you to see!

*programme's = programme is

7 Listen to the following sentences on the audio and repeat.

Notice that **than** and **as** are weak and are pronounced / ðən / and /əz /.
Other words have a strong stress such as: **News, Weather, isn't, Sports**.
Notice also that many words are linked.˘
The news˘is more interesting than the weather, but˘it˘isn't˘as˘interesting as˘a sports programme.

8 Listen to these similar sentences and repeat. Pay attention to sentence stress and linking.

a. A comedy is more exciting than a documentary, but it isn't as exciting as a horror movie.
b. A quiz is more educational than the weather, but it isn't as educational as a documentary.
c. A quiz is funnier than a documentary, but it isn't as funny as a comedy.
d. A documentary is more boring than the news, but it isn't as boring as the weather.
e. A movie is more relaxing than a sports programme, but it isn't as relaxing as a music programme.
f. An action movie is scarier than the news, but it isn't as scary as a horror movie.

GRAMMAR

Using adjectives to compare		2 things	More than 2 things
Short adjectives	small big	smaller bigger	smallest biggest
Adjectives ending in -y	funny scary	funnier scarier	funniest scariest
Adjectives with 2 syllables or more	relaxing exciting	more relaxing more exciting	most relaxing most exciting
Irregular adjectives	good bad	better worse	best worst

To describe an equal comparison you can use: …as…as…:

I like documentaries as much as I like comedies.

I watch TV as often as I listen to the radio.

You can use '…isn't as…as…' to describe unequal comparison:

A quiz is funnier than a documentary, but it isn't as funny as a comedy.

9 *Make sentences about each of the following pictures using the adjectives given and the comparison language above.*

Lin (age 11)

Jon (age 5)

May (age 12)

Adjectives: tall / young

Example: May is as tall as Lin, but she's taller than Jon.
Jon is younger than May and Lin. He's the youngest of them all.
Lin is younger than May, but she isn't as young as Jon.

Lin (age 7)

Jill (age 3)

Sam (age 12)

a. Adjectives: short / old

b. Adjectives: modern / old fashioned / popular

c. Adjectives: interesting / educational

Action movie	Comedy	Thriller

d. Adjectives: exciting / amusing / scary

Put it all together

10 In pairs, ask each other the following questions and fill in the gaps with your own answers.

1. Do you prefer movies to documentaries? Why?	Yes / No. I prefer ________ because they are ________ than ____________.
2. Which type of television programmes do you think young people like best? Why?	I think young people prefer ____________ ____________. They like them because ____________ ________.
3. Do you think you spend too much time watching television? What other activities could you do instead of watching television?	Yes / No / Maybe. I could ________________.
4. Are there other activities which are healthier than watching television? Why?	Yes / No / Maybe. They are healthier because__________. Or: They are as healthy ____________ because ________________.
5. Which is worse for children, spending too much time on the television or the computer?	I think spending too much time on the computer isn't as ________ ____ the television, but it ____________ ____________.
6. Which is more interesting for you, reading magazines or watching television?	I think ______________ isn't as ________ because ____________. Or: I think they are as interesting ___ each other because ______________.

Focus on Part 2 of the IELTS Speaking Test

11 Read the following Part 2 prompt card.

Describe a movie that you have seen and enjoyed.
You should talk about:
what the movie was called
when and where you saw it
what type of movie it was (comedy, action, romance, etc.)
and say why you enjoyed it.

In the IELTS exam you have one minute to make quick notes about what you are going to say. Only write main words in your notes.

For example:

'Talk about why you enjoyed it.'
Your notes = Good story, famous actor, very good looking, lots of action

12 Use these prompts to help you make quick notes before you speak.

Prompt	Your notes
What was the movie called?	
When and where did you see it? (If you can't remember, tell the examiner. This is fine.)	
What type of movie was it?	
Why did you enjoy it?	

13 Speak for half a minute, or longer if you can, about this topic to your partner. Use your notes to make longer sentences. Remember to use the same verb tense as the prompt card. For example:

The movie **was** called .... I **saw** it...... (past simple tense)

Focus on Part 3 of the IELTS Speaking Test

In Part 3 of the IELTS exam, the examiner asks questions to test whether you can speak about more complex topics that are connected to the Part 2 topic.

For example:

'150 years **ago** there were no radios, televisions or computers. What do you think people used to do in their free time?'

14 Write down some ideas. Use your dictionary if you need to. Tell your partner your ideas.

What about the future? In 50 years time, do you think we will watch television and listen to the radio? What about newspapers? Will people still read them?

15 Tell your partner what you think will happen.

16 Listen to the audio of an examiner asking a candidate some questions. Fill in the gaps as you listen.

Examiner: What type of activities did people do in their free time before the invention of radios, televisions and computers?

Candidate: I think in the olden days people __________ ____ spend their free time reading or doing activities with their __________. Fathers __________ _____teach their sons to make things out of __________ and mothers _________ ___ teach their _____________ to sew. People probably _______________ games too, such as chess and mahjong.

Examiner: Do you think this was a better way of life compared to how we live nowadays?

Candidate: In some ways it was better. Families ___________ more time talking together whereas today we __________ more time watching television or playing on the computer. I guess the parents ___________ the children in the olden days, but nowadays children learn a lot by themselves from the computer and television.

Examiner: In 50 years time, do you think things will change much or will we be doing the same activities as now in our free time?

Candidate: In my opinion, I believe we will change. I think people _______ see the benefits of spending more time talking together and less time by ___________ in front of a computer or television. Maybe more electronic, educational games ________ be ____________ that need three or four people to play them, like Play Station games, and the whole family _______ be able to play together.

17 *Look at the script. What grammatical structures do the speakers use when talking about past activities?*

Past simple verbs

Families spent more time talking

Did + subject + base verb? when asking a question about the past.

What type of activities did people do in their free time?

Used to + base verb when talking about a past habit or state that no longer happens.

I think in the olden days people used to spend their free time…

18 *In pairs, practise asking and answering the following questions using the structures given.*

Question 1: ***used to***

What do you think your grandmother _______________________ (do) in her free time?

Answer: She _________________________

Question 2: ***past simple***

What _________ you ____ (do) in your free time yesterday?

Answer: Yesterday, I ______________

Question 3: ***used to***

Did your father or mother ______________________ (spend) time teaching you things when you were a child?
Answer: ____.

Look at the script. What grammatical structure do the speakers use when talking about future possibilities or predictions?

Will + base verb

In 50 years time, do you think things will change much?
I think people will see the benefits…

19 *In pairs, practise asking and answering the following questions using this structure* 'will + base form.' *Choose either the verb* 'have' *or* 'be' *for each sentence.*

Remember: **'have'** is followed by a noun phrase and '**be**' is followed by an adjective.

Q 1: Do you think you ______________________ a good job in 15 years time?
Answer: Yes /No. I think I ______________ a ______________
(e.g.: doctor, policeman, mother, cleaner)

Q 2: Do you think you ____________________ children/grandchildren in 15 years time?
Answer: ____

Q 3: Do you think any member of your family ______________ famous?
Answer: ____

FLUENCY AND COHERENCE

20 *With a partner read the script above. One person is the examiner and the other the candidate.*

21 *Ask each other the same questions as in the script but this time answer in your own words with your own opinion. Try not to copy the script's answers.*

Remember to use **past simple** to talk about the past and **will + base form** to talk about future possibilities.

a. What type of activities did people do in their free time before the invention of radios, televisions and computers?
b. Do you think this was a better way of life compared to how we live nowadays?
c. In 50 years time, do you think things will change much or will we do the same activities in our free time?

Speaking

UNIT 5 Relationships

Focus on Part 2 of the IELTS Speaking Test

WARM-UP

1 Listen to the audio recording and repeat the words in the box.

mother	father	grandmother	grandfather	uncle	aunt	cousin	brother	sister

2 Listen again and mark the stressed syllable in each word.

For example:

grandmother

3 Finish labeling the family tree diagram below with words from the box.

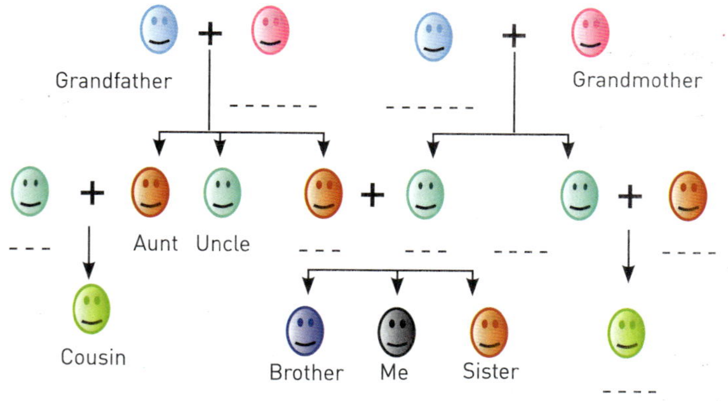

4 Now, make the family tree diagram a picture of your family by adding or deleting information.

5 Look at your partner's diagram and ask for information.

Example: A. Tell me about your grandmother.
B. Well, she's very kind and generous. She's a great cook, too.

*In your answer, give at least **two** pieces of information about each member of the family.*

VOCABULARY

Vocabulary Bank

Family / relatives

parent(s)
son
daughter
grandparent(s)
grandson
granddaughter
niece
nephew
cousin
son-in-law
daughter-in-law
mother-in-law
father-in-law
sister-in-law
brother-in-law
step mother
stepfather
stepsister
stepbrother

girlfriend
boyfriend
partner[1]

an only child
baby / infant
toddler
teenager
adult / grownup

childhood
adolescence
adulthood

nuclear family
extended family

to separate
to divorce
to remarry

Describing family / friends

Physical characteristics

short, tall, fat, thin etc.
good-looking
attractive
handsome
pretty
beautiful

Qualities, personality, nature, character

sociable
shy
outgoing
adventurous
amusing
intelligent
competitive
cheerful
pessimistic
optimistic
helpful
(in)considerate
sensitive
stubborn
caring
supportive
brave
funny
humorous
patient
honest
trustworthy
generous
thoughtful
kind
loyal
faithful
reliable

add more words ...

Collocations

to bring up a child

to get on (well) with

to have a good / close relationship with someone

a relationship between two people

to start a relationship

to end a relationship

to be similar to

to be different from

to have (something / a lot) in common with someone
>We have a lot in common.
>We don't have much in common.
>I have a lot in common with my sister.

to have the same tastes in something

to have different tastes in something
>We have the same tastes in clothes but we have different tastes in music.

add more phrases of your own...

[1] We use this word for an **adult** boyfriend or girlfriend.

6 *Study the words in the* ***Vocabulary Bank****.*

7 *Tick ✓ the words you know.*

Highlight or underline the unfamiliar words and then look them up in a dictionary.

8 *Fill in the gaps with words or phrases from the 'Family / relatives' section of the* ***Vocabulary Bank****.*

a. My mother's sister is my __________.
b. My father's sister is my __________.
c. My cousin's father is my __________.
d. My mother's father is my __________.
e. My mother's sister has two children, a boy and a girl. They are my mother's __________ and __________.
f. I don't have any brothers or sisters. I am ________________________.
g. My uncle and his wife don't live together any more. They are __________.
h. __________ can be a difficult stage in life. You are no longer a child but not yet an adult.
i. My youngest cousin is just learning to walk. She is a __________.
j. My aunt is divorced but she is dating again. She has a new __________.

PRONUNCIATION

Word Stress

9 *Listen to the audio recording and repeat the words in the box. These are useful words for describing people.*

cheerful	considerate	adventurous	stubborn	pessimistic
outgoing	amusing	sociable	pleasant	shy

10 *How many syllables are there in each word?*

For example:

cheer-ful = 2 syllables

11 *Listen to the words again. Mark the stressed syllable, and then match each word with a stress pattern:*

For example:

cheerful = pattern 2

Pattern 1 = O
Pattern 2 = Oo
Pattern 3 = oOo
Pattern 4 = Ooo
Pattern 5 = oOoo
Pattern 6 = ooOo

12 Practise saying the words after the model. Be sure to say the stressed syllable slightly louder and longer.

GRAMMAR

Contractions

*13 Listen to a student talking about the topic **Family**.*

I'd like to tell you about my family. I have two brothers. They're both at university. The older one is studying computer science and the younger one is studying economics. My parents are divorced. My father has remarried and lives with my stepmother and her three children, two sons and a daughter. My stepbrothers also like computers but my stepsister prefers reading books. I have a good relationship with my stepsister because we've got a lot in common. I read lots of books too and we like to discuss the ideas that we've read in them. Unfortunately, I don't get on well with my stepmother. She doesn't like me very much and we often argue. The relationship between my older brother and me is very close. We've shared many adventures together at weekends and on holidays. We play the same sports as well. The person in my family that I have the best relationship with is my mother. She's a very cheerful and considerate person and I love her very much.

Note: When speaking, **contractions** sound more natural.

For example:

I am > I'm
I would > I'd

14 Look at the tape script and underline all the contractions.

Position of also and both.

When we use the adverb **also** in the middle of a sentence:

- If the verb is one word, **also** goes *before* the verb.
  My stepbrothers **also** *like* computers.
  She reads books and **also** *discusses* them.
- **Also** goes *after* the verb *to be (am/is/are/was/were)*.
  They are clever but they *are* **also** naughty.
- If the verb is two or more words, **also** goes *after* the *first verb*.

My younger brother *can* **also** *dance* hip-hop.
My grandparents *have* **also** *been* to Japan.
Do you **also** *like* reading?

- We use both in the same way:
  My parents **both** *work*.
  Jin and Su *are* **both** at university.
  They *are* **both** studying economics.

15 Look at the prompt card below and then close your book and see if you can remember the key points.

Describe your best friend.
You should say:
 who he/she is
 when you first met
 why you became friends
and explain how you spend your time together.

16 Now write some key words for each point.

Who: ....

When: ....

Why: because ....

Spend time: doing ....

playing ....

going ....

17 With your partner listening, try to talk for at least half a minute.

18 Listen to the audio recording of a student talking on this topic.

Script of 'Best friend' topic

I'm going to tell you about my best friend, Lou An. We first met a few years ago at the local athletics club. She's not really good-looking or anything, but she is very helpful and thoughtful and she has a really cheerful and outgoing personality. We are about the same age and we have a lot in common so I guess that's the main reason we became friends. Of course we both love sport, especially running and cycling. She's very competitive, much more competitive than I am. She exercises for an hour or two every day. We also have similar tastes in movies and television programmes. She loves romantic comedies and so do I. She probably watches more sport on television than I do, though. When we are together we mostly spend our time playing sport, obviously, or shopping for clothes. When we go to the shopping mall, we often don't buy anything but it's fun just looking at the different styles of the new clothes and trying them on. It's good to have a reliable friend with you who will give you her honest opinion. Sometimes we go to the beach or the swimming pool together although neither of us can swim very well. Nowadays, we both seem to be very busy but we still meet at least once a week for a chat, usually on Friday afternoons. We generally go to a cafe and have something to drink. It's funny, though, our tastes are quite different in this case. Whereas I prefer coffee, she never drinks coffee. She only drinks tea.

19 *Look at the script, identify and underline all the adjectives from the 'Qualities' list in the* ***Vocabulary Bank****.*

20 *Fill in the gaps with suitable adjectives taken from the box.*

Note: there are more words in the box than you need and there may be more than one correct answer for each gap.

trustworthy	thoughtful	supportive	sociable
shy	reliable	patient	outgoing
generous	considerate	cheerful	caring
brave	adventurous	kind	honest

a. He enjoys unusual and rather dangerous activities like white-water rafting. He's so ______.
b. He's also very ______. If he hurts himself, he never complains about the pain.
c. They gave a lot of money to the earthquake victims. They're ______.
d. IELTS examiners are very ______. They are quite calm even if they have to repeat the same question three times.
e. My father is very ______. When he says he'll do something, he always does it.
f. My aunt has lots of fun at parties because she is so ______ and ______.
g. A good friend should be ______ and always tell the truth.
h. My youngest cousin isn't very good at talking to new people. She's quite ______.
i. Their mother is ______ and ______. She's a helpful person who understands other people's needs and problems.

21 *Give another talk about* ***Your Best Friend*** *including some words and phrases from the 'Qualities' list in the Vocabulary Bank.*

Focus on Part 3 of the IELTS Speaking Test

After you have talked about your topic in Part 2, the examiner will ask you some more **general** questions about the topic. These questions are more abstract and may not be directly related to your experience.
Example: Part 2 topic = Best friend

→ Part 3 topic = Relationships

Let's talk about friendship in general. How important is it for people to have friends?

Well, I think having friends is extremely important...

What personal qualities do you think a real friend should have?

I think there are a number of qualities that a real friend has...

Would you say that friends are more important than family?

Definitely, because we spend more time with friends and ...

Now, let's move on to talk about how people form relationships. Nowadays more and more people are starting relationships on the Internet. What are the advantages of forming a relationship in this way? What are the dangers?

Well, the main advantage is that starting a relationship on the Internet is so easy...

Do you think Internet relationships can ever be as strong as traditional relationships?

Well, it depends on what kind of relationship it is and...

How are relationships formed in childhood different from those formed in adolescence and adulthood?

Well, I think childhood relationships are ...

FLUENCY AND COHERENCE

Emphasis in Opening Statements

22 *Listen to the audio recording and underline the word or syllable that carries the main stress in these introductory phrases in italics.*

23 *Listen again and practise saying the opening statements with appropriate emphasis.*

For example:

Well, I think...

24 *Now, try answering the examiner's questions above by completing the statements in the candidate's speech bubbles.*

For example:

Well, I think having friends is extremely important because everyone needs someone to talk to about their problems.

25 *Listen to the model Part 3 Discussion on Relationships below.*

Examiner: 'Well, you've been talking about a special friend, and now I'd like to go on to talk with you some more about relationships in general. First of all, let's talk about friendship in general. How important is it for people to have friends?'

Candidate: '**Well, I think** having friends is extremely important because everyone needs someone to talk to about their problems; not only that, but we need people to share the good times with as well. I can't imagine how lonely it would be if we didn't have any friends.'

Examiner: 'What personal qualities do you think a real friend should have?'

Candidate: '**I think there are a number of qualities** that a real friend has. Firstly, friends should be honest and trustworthy because you tell them your secrets and personal details, you know, really private stuff. You have to be able to trust them. Secondly, I think they should be reliable. They should meet you when they say they're going to and not let you down. I also think friends should be caring and supportive so they listen to you when you tell them your troubles and so they help you if you need help. I guess it's also more fun if they are cheerful and amusing.'

Examiner: 'Would you say that friends are more important than family?'

Candidate: '**Definitely, because** we spend more time with friends and they can have a huge influence on us. Sometimes that can be a bad influence, so we need to choose our friends carefully.'

Examiner: 'Now let's move on to talk about how people form relationships. Nowadays more and more people are starting relationships on the Internet. What are the advantages of forming a relationship in this way?'

Candidate: '**Well, the main advantage is** that starting a relationship on the Internet is so easy. Even if you are a really shy person, and not very sociable, you can still find friends on the Internet. I think some people find it much, much easier than face to face talking.'

Examiner: 'What are the dangers?'

Candidate: '**It seems to me that** Internet relationships are not really dangerous unless you agree to meet the person and that person has been dishonest, you know, pretending to be someone else... telling lies about himself. This is easy to do on the Internet. I know this happens sometimes because I've read about it in the newspaper ... but it's never happened to me.'

Examiner: 'Do you think Internet relationships can ever be as strong as traditional relationships?'

Candidate: '**I think it depends on** the kind of relationship. Before the Internet, people used to have pen friends. They wrote letters to each other and sometimes those pen friends became very close and that can also happen on the Internet.'

Examiner: 'Are relationships formed in childhood different from those formed in adolescence and adulthood?'

Candidate: '**Yes, I think so**. Children like to play with their friends, but adolescents just like to hang out with their friends and talk a lot. I guess adults make friends at work.'

Examiner: 'Thank you.'

26 *In pairs, ask and answer the examiner's questions. This time, try to give your own views but you may find it helpful to use words, phrases or ideas from the dialogue. Remember to use an opening statement to begin your answer.*

Speaking

UNIT 6 Advertising

Focus on Part 2 of the IELTS Speaking Test

WARM-UP

1 *Look at these different places where we see and hear advertising. Work with a partner to add some more.*

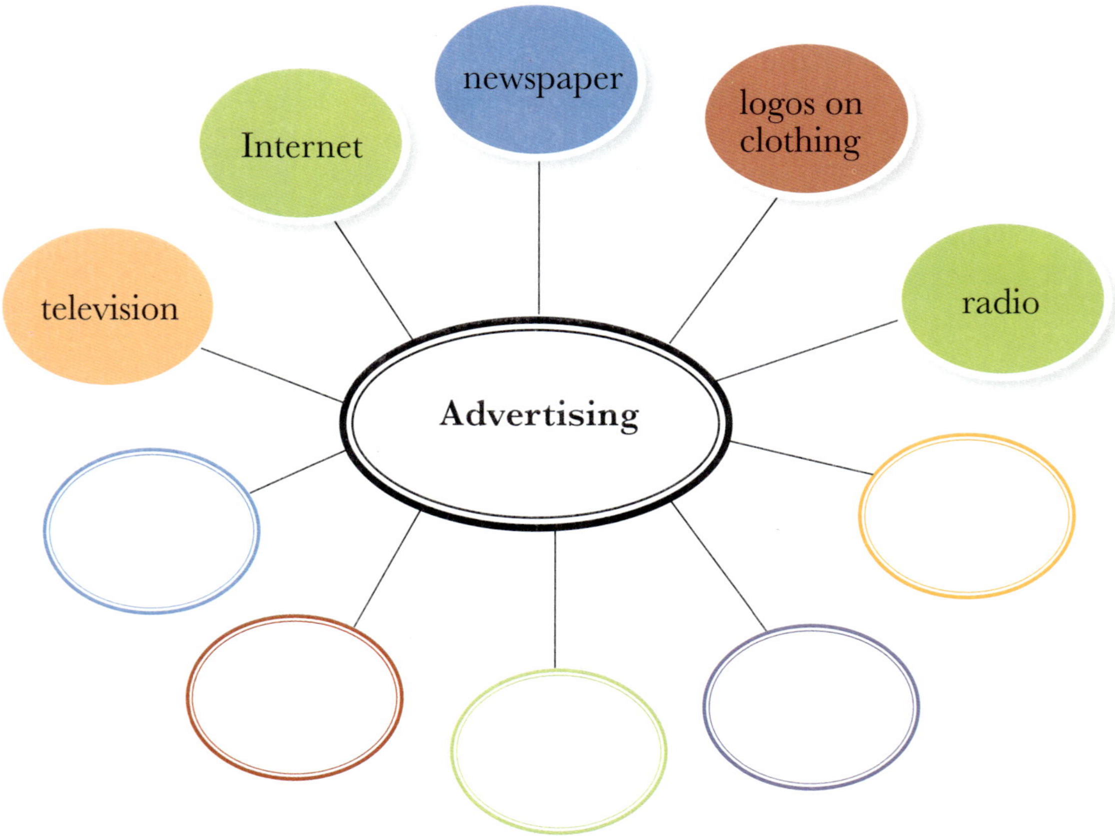

In each of the above places, advertisements convey their messages in different ways, for example, paper, print, colour, music, words, images and sound.

2 *With a partner, think about all the different ways each place uses to display advertisements. Complete the table using your ideas. The first three have been done for you as examples.*

Place	Means
television	sound (talking, music, sound effects), moving images, colour, written words, still images
newspaper	paper, print, words, photos, colour, black and white
logos on clothing	caps, sweatshirts, t-shirts, print, colour, images, words, brand names
Internet	
radio	

3 *Listen to the following speakers discussing advertisements they have seen. Circle the place where they saw the ad.*

a.	cinema	television	Internet
b.	brochure	magazine	clothing
c.	television	radio	Internet
d.	poster	brochure	magazine
e.	banner	clothing	newspaper

VOCABULARY

Vocabulary Bank				
Advertising			Attitudes & Opinions	Phrases & Collocations
Nouns	Verbs	Adjectives		
advertisement (= advert or ad)	advertise	accurate	amazing	black and white photo
actor	appear	bold	amusing	brand name
banner	convey	bright	annoying	colour photo
billboard	display	catchy	awful	sandwich board
brand	influence	colourful	cheesy	self-esteem
brochure	persuade	distinctive	cute	sound effects
cartoon	seem	elegant	entertaining	target audience
cinema	show	humorous	ethical	visual effects
clothing	target	imaginary	exciting	
flyer		informative	funny	• to advertise a product
image		loud	great	• to catch your attention
jingle		misleading	memorable	• to convey a message
logo		musical	professional	• to display a logo
magazine		original	responsible	• to hand out flyers / brochures
media		real-life	strange	• to pay attention to
model		recent	terrible	• to play an advert on TV / on the radio
print		serious	unethical	• to put up a poster / a banner
product			unprofessional	• to stand out
sign				
slogan				
stationery				
television (= TV)				

4 *Think of five different advertisements you've seen or heard recently. Brainstorm each one and write words in the correct columns below. Use the vocabulary bank and your dictionary to help you.*

Where did you see the ad?	What was it for?	What was it like?	Why do you remember it?
e.g. television	e.g. a brand of running shoes	e.g. colourful, cartoon images, musical	e.g. funny cartoon, annoying jingle
1.			
2.			
3.			
4.			
5.			

5 *Now compare your lists of words with a partner. Do you both have some of the same words? Have you both seen some of the same ads?*

PRONUNCIATION

Weak and strong forms — *can* and *can't*

In English, there are many small 'grammar' words that have both a weak and a strong form. The weak form is the form that is most commonly used when we speak. The strong form is used when we say the word on its own, or when we want to emphasize the word in a sentence.

6 *Listen to the two forms of 'can'. Decide which one is weak and which one is strong.*

a. weak strong
b. weak strong

The vowel sound is different in the weak form and the strong form. In the strong form, the 'a' sounds like it does at the beginning of the word 'apple' /æ/. In the weak form, it sounds like the short sound at the end of the word 'China' /ə/.

7 *Listen and repeat. Focus on the sounds of the letter 'a'.*

a. c<u>a</u>n <u>a</u>pple <u>a</u>dvertising c<u>a</u>n
b. you c<u>a</u>n see in Chin<u>a</u> in the medi<u>a</u> you c<u>a</u>n see

8 *Now listen and repeat the sentences. Focus on imitating the form of 'can' that you hear.*

a. Yes, I <u>can</u> see it.
b. You <u>can</u> see it on TV.

Unlike 'can', '**can't**' does **not** have a weak form. It has the same vowel sound, whether it is stressed or unstressed in a sentence.

9 *Listen and decide if 'can't' is stressed or unstressed in the following sentences.*

a) unstressed stressed
b) unstressed stressed

You probably noticed that the 'a' in 'can't' sounds like the 'a' in 'dance' or 'chance' /a:/.

10 Listen and repeat. Focus on the sound of the letter 'a'.

can't dance chance can't

11 Now listen and repeat the sentences. Focus on imitating the form of 'can't' that you hear.

a. I can't understand why not.
b. You can't see it on TV.

GRAMMAR

In spoken English, native speakers usually use **contractions**, the shortened forms of certain words.

12 Work with a partner. Look at these contractions. Do you know the long forms?

Contraction	Long form
can't	________________
isn't	________________
don't	________________
didn't	________________
she's	________________

13 Listen and check your answers. Then listen and repeat.

14 Look at these long forms. Do you know the contractions?

Contraction	Long form
________________	**does not**
________________	**will not**
________________	**they are**
________________	**it is**
________________	**are not**

15 Listen and check your answers. Then listen and repeat.

16 Now listen and complete the sentences by writing a contraction in each space.

a. You ________________ see the people because it's a radio ad.
b. In the picture, ________________ wearing a funny costume.
c. ________________ been an interesting ad in the paper recently.
d. There ________________ any colour; ________________ completely black and white.
e. ________________ a group of people in colourful clothes, and ________________ all laughing.

17 For each of the sentences above, write the long form of the contraction(s).

a. ____________________

b. ____________________

c. ____________________

d. ____________________; ____________________

e. ____________________; ____________________

Put it all together

Look at the topic card below.

Describe an advertisement that you have seen / heard recently.

You should say:

what it was for

where you saw / heard it

what it was like

and explain why you remember it.

18 Think of an advertisement that you have seen or heard recently. For each of the points listed on the card, note down the words and phrases you will need.

19 Listen to a candidate talking on this topic. As you listen, choose the right answer.

a. What was the advertisement for?
   toilet cleaner / toilet paper / children's toys

b. Where did the speaker see / hear the advertisement?
   television / radio / Internet

c. What was it like?
   serious / informative / humorous

d. Why does the speaker remember it?
   the elegant music / the classical music / the rock music

20 Listen to the recording again. Look at the prompt card and make notes below.

* What the ad was for:

* Where I saw / heard it:

* What it was like:

* I remember it because:

Focus on Part 3 of the IELTS Speaking Test

In Part 3 of the speaking test, you will be asked to give your opinion.

21 *Look at the following questions and circle the word that best expresses your own opinion.*

What do you think about?

a. advertisements that target children and young teenagers?
   I think that they're... good okay bad
b. advertisements that use very thin models?
   I think that they're... good okay bad
c. advertisements that don't show the true price of the product or service?
   I think that they're... good okay bad
d. advertisements that make the product/service appear better than it actually is?
   I think that they're... good okay bad

22 *When you have finished, compare your answers with a partner. Do you agree?*

23 *Listen to a candidate talking about the same questions. Go back and underline the word that best expresses her opinion.*

24 *Listen again and complete the phrases that show she's giving her opinion. The first one has been done for you.*

a. I don't think it's...
b. In ________ ________, these...
c. I ________ ________ it's...
d. I ________ ________ it's...

FLUENCY AND COHERENCE

25 *Look at the questions again and answer them using the information given below and the opinion phrases from above. Work with a partner.*

a.
What do you think about advertisements that target children and young teenagers?
It's not very ethical.

b.
What do you think about advertisements that use very thin models?
These kinds of ads are largely responsible for the low self-esteem of many young girls and women.

c.

What do you think about advertisements that don't show the true price of the product or service?

I don't believe it's always possible to show the true price.

d.

What do you think about advertisements that make the product or service appear better than it actually is?

It's not that bad.

26 *Use the ideas given below and the phrases in the box to give an opinion. The first one has been done for you as an example.*

I think... / I don't think...	I believe... / I don't believe...
I feel... / I don't feel...	In my opinion...

a. Big companies spend too much money on advertising.

'I don't believe that advertising really influences what people buy.'

b. Television advertising reaches more people than print media.

....

c. Children can persuade their parents to buy things.

....

d. Many radio advertisements aren't very professional.

....

27 *Look at the following questions. Note down all of the vocabulary items you will need to give your own opinion. Use the Vocabulary Bank and your dictionary to help you if necessary.*

a. What do you think about advertisements that target children and young teenagers?
b. What do you think about advertisements that use very thin models?
c. What do you think about advertisements that don't show the true price of the product or service?
d. What do you think about advertisements that make the product or service appear better than it actually is?
e. Do you think that advertising can have a negative influence on children?
f. Do you think that the amount some companies spend on advertising is excessive?
g. Do you think television advertising is more effective than print media?

28 *Now work with a partner. Take turns to ask and answer the questions above. Make sure that you give your own opinion.*

UNIT 7 Further Study and Future Plans

Focus on Part 1 of the IELTS Speaking Test

WARM-UP

1 *Listen and repeat the following Part 1 questions*

i. Right, let's talk about what you do. Do you work or are you a student?
ii. What subjects are you studying?
iii. Is biology a difficult subject?
iv. What's the most interesting aspect of biology?
v. What's the least interesting aspect of biology?

2 *Match the candidate's answers to the questions above.*

a. I'm studying biology, English, maths, physics and chemistry.
b. No, I don't find it difficult, because I enjoy studying science and I have a really good teacher.
c. I guess the most boring part of biology is learning all the names for things, because you have to learn them over and over to remember them.
d. I'm a student at high school.
e. The most interesting aspect? I think it's how biology applies to people and everyday life.

TIP

Notice in answer (e), the student repeats part of the question in his answer. This is a good way to clarify the question and it also makes your speaking more natural. You can make your voice go up at the end of the phrase, to make it sound like a question. Don't use this strategy with every question though!

3 *Student A: You are the examiner. Use the Part 1 questions from the warm-up to ask your partner.*

Student B: You are the candidate. Give your own answers to the questions.

4 *Change roles and repeat the exercise.*

Focus on Part 2 of the IELTS Speaking Test

Describe a course or subject you would like to take in the future.
You should say:
 what the course is
 what is involved e.g. cost, length of time, what is taught, etc.
 where you would study
and why it is that you want to take the course or study this subject.

There are two main ways you could answer this Part 2 question:

- Talk about an academic course or qualification you would like to study in the future, such as a diploma at university.
- Talk about a short course or class you would like to do for fun, such as learning how to ski or learning to play the guitar.

Firstly, let's take a closer look at the first option.

5 *Look at these key words from the candidate's long turn that you will listen to soon. What do you think he will talk about? Tell your partner your predictions.*

MBA	Australia/NZ/	dream	expensive
run a business	English	reputable	get ahead

Now listen to the candidate's long turn and number the words from above as you hear them mentioned.

a.________ b.________ c.________

d.________ e.________ f.________

g.________ h.________

When you finish your long turn, the examiner will ask one or two questions related to what you have spoken about. These are called 'rounding off' questions.

6 *Listen to the next part of the audio where the examiner asks two rounding off questions.*

Examiner: After you completed your MBA studies, do you think you would want to do further study?
Candidate: Ah, no…I think that would be enough. I will need to make some money after that!
Examiner: Yes. And, do you normally find it easy or difficult to learn new things?

Candidate: Um, it depends. I think it depends on whether I am interested in what I am learning or not. How motivated I am, you know...

Examiner: Thank you.

TIP
Listen carefully when the examiner says: "Thank you." This indicates the end of Part 2

VOCABULARY

7 *Look at the useful vocabulary from the speaker. Check the meanings in your dictionary.*

goal	get ahead	reputable
successful	undergraduate degree	master's degree
university	to run	motivated

8 *Mark the stressed syllables in each word.*

9 *Listen and repeat the words.*

10 *Choose the best word or phrase from the chart above to fill in the gaps.*

a. Candy is extremely ______________ to pass her IELTS test with band 7, because she wants to study art in London. She works very hard on her English.

b. Oxford University in England is very ____________________. It has a long history of excellent education and is well known all over the world.

c. Joe's main _________ this year is to get good marks on his end of year exams.

d. My professor thinks the top ______________ in China is Tsinghua, because students who study there have an excellent pass rate.

e. Diana wants to pass her Master's degree so she can be promoted and _____________ the advertising department at her job.

f. Finn is studying his ______________ at South China Agricultural University, but he hopes to study his ____________ at Auckland University in New Zealand.

g. She has been quite _________________________ at studying languages — she speaks English, Mandarin, Korean and Greek!

h. Grant knew he had to ______________ of the other students in his class, so he started taking extra English classes in order to be better than his classmates.

Vocabulary Bank		
Other ways to express 'knowledge or skill'	**To express future desire (verb)**	**To express a future desire (noun)**
aptitude	to aim	aim
be acquainted with	to aspire to	ambition
be aware of	to fancy	aspiration
be familiar with	to pursue	goal
be proficient in	to set (one's) heart on	intention
be up on	to yearn	objective
expertise		
have a knowledge of		
have the ability		
have the know-how		
have the skill		

PRONUNCIATION

In spoken English, rhythm is important. Rhythm is the combination of stressed and unstressed syllables.

11 Read this sentence from the warm-up activity:

I'm a student at high school.

ooOooOo
I'maSTUdentatHIGHschool
DedeDAdedeDAde

12 Listen and repeat the sentence, paying attention to the stress and rhythm.

13 Say the other phrases from exercise 2 of this unit with the correct stress and rhythm.

*14 Listen to the other phrases in the previous Part 1 warm-up. Can you write the stress and rhythm of each phrase in the boxes below? Write **o** for the weak syllables and **O** for the stressed syllables in each phrase. The first one has been done for you.*

PHRASE	STRESS
I'm studying biology, English, maths, physics and chemistry.	OooooOoo, Oo, O,OooOoo
I don't find it difficult, because I enjoy studying science.	
I have a good teacher.	
The most interesting aspect?	
I think it's how biology applies to people and everyday life.	

15 Listen and repeat each answer. As you speak, tap out the rhythm quietly on your desk with your finger or pencil.

GRAMMAR

You can use different ways to talk about future goals in English. Look at these sentences from the speaker:

I would love to take an MBA course in the future.

I would love to + base verb + time marker

I hope to run my own business some day.

I hope to + base verb + time marker

You can also use the following language:

One of my goals is to study overseas.

One of my dreams is to be a millionaire!

One of my goals/dreams + to + base verb

I aim to learn Spanish one day.

I aim to + base verb + time marker

16 Think about your own academic goals for the future. Write your sentences below using the verbs given in brackets.

(hope)________________________________

(aim)________________________________

(dream)________________________________

(would love to) ____________________________

(goal) ________________________________

17 Using the sentence starters below, make short notes to prepare for your long turn.

18 Work in pairs and speak for up to one minute using these sentences starters.

A course I would love to take in the future is...

The course involves studying...

It takes about ...years

The reason I want to study this course is because...

Remember we said there were two main ways of answering the Part 2 topic card in this unit? Now let's look at the second option:

Talking about something you would like to learn for fun or interest

19 Listen to the speaker talking.

a. What does she want to learn how to do?
b. Is it easy or difficult?

Describe a course, subject or class you would like to take in the future.
You should say:
What the course is
What is involved
Where you would study
and why it is that you want to take the course or study this subject.

20 Look at the underlined words in the script. Can you guess the meaning of these two words from their context? Write a short definition and check with your partner.

gear (**n**):______________________________

take up (**v**):______________________________

'I'd really like to learn to surf. Whenever I see people out on the water, they look like they are having so much fun! So there is a course that I've found, which you can just do for a day down on the coast. They give you all the **gear** that you need, you know, like a wetsuit and a surfboard and so on, and they run classes the whole day. They actually teach you on the beach and in the water. I think they teach you how to balance on the surfboard, how to paddle, how to keep safe and how to stand up on the board, of course! Then after that you can choose to sign up for a longer course, which runs every Saturday. I've talked to some people who've done it, and they say the tutors are friendly and professional. It's one of my dreams to be able to surf because I love the sea, and I love swimming, so surfing feels like the next step. And it looks so exciting, plus it's such a good way to keep fit. And all the cute boys go surfing! But people say it's really difficult and takes a lot of time, effort and practice, so I might have to wait until I've finished my exams for this year, and **take up** surfing in summer.'

21 What type of courses and new skills would you like to take up for fun?

- A new skill, e.g. web design
- A creative hobby, e.g. photography
- A sport, e.g. snowboarding
- A useful skill, e.g. cooking
- A musical instrument, e.g. guitar
- An artistic skill, e.g. dancing

22 Use the following questions to help you prepare short notes for your own answer. In pairs, practise your long turn answer.

Which type of course/classes would you take?	
What would the classes teach you? (i.e. What is involved?)	
Where would you take the classes?	
Why do you want to take this course/class?	
ADDING EXTRA INFORMATION	
Do you need any special gear for your course/class?	
Do you think it would be difficult or easy to learn?	
Why?Have you heard anything about the course/class?	

Focus on Part 3 of the IELTS Speaking Test

FLUENCY AND COHERENCE

23 Sometimes, you will be unfamiliar with Part 3 vocabulary. If this is the case, you should try to guess and clarify the meaning for yourself. Below, the candidate does not know the word 'curriculum'. Listen to how she copes.

Examiner: Could you tell me how you think the high school curriculum has changed in your country since the last century?

Candidate: Oh, mmm, curriculum. Do you mean what we do at school? The different subjects we study?

Examiner: Yes. Subjects or courses of study.

Candidate: Well, actually I believe the school curriculum at high school has changed considerably. Students nowadays take subjects which didn't even exist at the beginning of last century, such as computer science.

24 Work in pairs.

a. Student A does activities 26, 27, and 28 below.
b. Student B does activities 29, 30 and 31 below.

Student A:

25 Look up the following words in your dictionary and write a synonym or brief definition:

Methods: ______________________
Status: ______________________
Gap year: ______________________

26 Now ask your partner the following Part 3 questions. If your partner does not know any of the underlined words, wait for him or her to guess the meaning before you give any help.

a. How do you think methods of teaching have changed over the last 100 years?
b. Is a university education considered high status in your country?
c. Do you think it is a good idea for students to have a 'gap year' between finishing high school and starting university?

27 Now answer your partner's questions.

Student B:

28 Look up the following words in your dictionary and write a synonym or brief definition:

Education system: ______________________
Alter: ______________________
Characteristics: ______________________

29 Now answer your partner's questions in Part 3. Guess the meaning of words you do not understand.

30 When you have answered the questions, ask your partner the following Part 3 questions. If your partner does not know any of the underlined words, wait for him or her to guess the meaning before you give any help.

a. How do you think the education system might change in the future?
b. If you could alter the education system in your country, what would you do?
c. In your opinion, what characteristics make a good teacher?

UNIT 8 The Natural Environment

Focus on Part 1 of the IELTS Speaking Test

WARM-UP

1 *Think of your home and answer the following questions.*

a. Do you live in a house, an apartment or another type of accommodation?
b. Are there any public facilities nearby e.g. a garden, sports park, library, and museum?
c. Is this a good area for old people, children or students? Why?
d. Describe the natural environment, e.g. nearby lakes or rivers, parks, and the air.

2 *Put the following vocabulary into the 2 lists, nouns or adjectives. The first ones have been done for you.*

traffic	beaches	mountains	suburban	stores
highways	crowded	seasons	historic	overcrowded
trees	weather	lake	park	path
picnic	population	pollution	polluted	environment
sprawling	industry	fall	grey and gloomy	clean

VOCABULARY

Nouns	Adjectives
• Traffic	• Suburban

3 *Use your dictionary to check the meaning of the words from the vocabulary list. Which words from the list have a negative meaning?*

4 *Listen to the words in exercise 2 and mark the stressed syllable in each word. Listen again and repeat the words.*

Vocabulary Bank

Places in the city	Cities can be described as ... (good / bad)	Negative effects on nature may be described as...
art gallery	bustling	appalling
boutique	congested	catastrophic
(pavement) cafe	dynamic	damaging
cathedral	historic	disastrous
cinema	lively	detrimental
department store	noisy	dreadful
fountain	overcrowded	endangered
market	overwhelming	harmful
museum	polluted	horrendous
nightclub	run-down	risky
skyscraper	smart	tragic
stadium	smoggy	unhealthy
subway	spectacular	
temple		
theatre		

PRONUNCIATION

l and r

5 *Listen to the audio and decide whether the speaker is saying the word in List A or List B. You'll hear each word twice. Place a tick beside the one you hear. The first one has been done for you.*

A		B		A		B		A		B	
light	√	right		playing		praying		lap		wrap	
lake		rake		lot		rot		lace		race	
lice		rice		lay		ray		lamp		ramp	
low		row		lane		rain		leap		reap	
long		wrong		lamb		ram		lock		rock	

6 *Listen and repeat the words above. Try practising these at home to hear the difference in the sounds and play the same game with your friends.*

7. *Listen to some candidates answering these Part 1 IELTS speaking questions. The answers are not in the correct order. Match the answers to the questions. The first one has been done or you.*

a. Where do you live? In an apartment or a house? Speaker 2
b. What is the area like where you live? ________
c. Describe the town or city where you live. ________
d. Where do people go at the weekend to enjoy some fresh air? ________
e. Describe a popular destination near your town which has natural beauty. ________

8 *Listen to the following Part 1 IELTS questions and mark the sentence stress. The first one has been done for you.*

a. Where do you <u>live</u>? In an a<u>part</u>ment or a <u>house</u>?
b. What is the area like where you live?
c. Describe the town or city where you live.
d. Where do people go at the weekend to enjoy some fresh air?
e. How do people enjoy the outdoors where you live?

9 *Work with a partner. Student A is the examiner and Student B is the candidate. Student A asks the questions above focusing on sentence stress. Student B chooses and reads the correct answer from the script at the end of this unit. Change roles and repeat.*

GRAMMAR

10 *Listen to find out what people can do to help the environment. Then answer the questions below.*

a. Who wants to reduce their impact on the environment?
b. Who thinks it's a good idea to drive less and use less electricity at home?
c. Who thinks that recycling uses too much energy and produces more carbon in the environment?
d. Who comments on the amount of waste people just throw on the ground?
e. Who recommends changing our lifestyle drastically?

11 What advice does Chloe give?

a. We ought to recycle some goods.
b. We should try to reuse things instead.

12 Can you exchange **should** *and* **ought to** *in these sentences without changing the meaning?*

Yes. Should and ought to have the ________ meaning for advice and conclusions:

SHOULD—OUGHT TO

We should not build any more roads through it.

We ought to do things to encourage nature lovers to visit the forest.

should and **ought to** have the same meaning.

You can always use **should** instead of **ought to**.

They are used when giving advice.

Pronunciation: should /ʃud/ weak form /ʃəd/

ought to /tu:/ weak form /tə/

Positive: Subject + should/ought to + base form verb

Negative: Subject + should + not + base form

Question: Should + subject + base form…?

Note: Questions and negative forms using 'ought to' are less common.

13 Listen to the audio and repeat. You'll hear each sentence twice.

a. You should try to cut down your carbon footprint.
b. You ought to travel by bike or on foot instead of car whenever possible.
c. We oughtn't to leave the lights on when we leave the room.
d. We shouldn't waste water.

14 Now read the scripts below and underline the words 'should' and 'ought to'.

Maddi

To try to cut down on our carbon footprint for the environment, we should travel by bike or on foot instead of using the car whenever possible. We also ought to turn lights off when we leave a room, take shorter showers to conserve water and recycle for sure!

Chloe

We ought to recycle some goods. People think that recycling is so good for the environment, but the truth is, it really isn't that great. You have to use fossil fuels for the energy to break it down and then make a new product out of it. We ought to try to reuse things instead.

Stacy

I've always thought we should go back to the basics. If everyone would quit throwing trash on the ground it would be a huge step in the right direction...Sounds simple, but drive down a highway and look to your left and right and you'll see what I mean

Michael

I think we should all sell our cars, our houses, and most belongings. Live in a brush hut, eat berries, wear leaves for clothes, and move every 2 months.

15 *Look at the script of the four speakers again and make sentences of their ideas using '**should**' or '**ought to**'. Write your sentences below. The first two have been done for you.*

a. You **ought to** cut down on your carbon footprint.

b. We **should** travel by bike or on foot instead of using the car whenever possible.

c. ....

d. ....

e. ....

f. ....

g. ....

h. ....

i. ....

j. ....

16 *Add some of your own ideas as to what people can do to help the environment. Start your sentences using '**I think we should/ought to...**' or '**In my opinion, we should/ought to...**'. Tell your partner your ideas.*

Put it all together

17 *Use the box below to write notes about the environment where you live. Make as many notes as possible. Use your dictionary and the vocabulary you have learnt in this unit.*

The Natural Environment	
Questions	**Notes for Answers**
Do you live in an apartment or a house?	
What is the area like where you live?	
Are there any parks or gardens nearby?	
Tell me about the town or city where you live.	
Where do people go at the weekend to enjoy some fresh air?	
How do people enjoy the outdoors where you live?	

18 Work in pairs. Ask and answer the questions above.

19 Here are some more questions for you to practise with.

a. Do you like spending time outdoors? Why/ Why not?
b. What activities do you enjoy outside? Why?
c. Are there any outdoor activities you don't enjoy? Why not?
d. Do you think being outside during the day is important? Why/Why not?
e. Describe a park or public garden that you enjoy visiting.
f. Where is a very popular place for people to go and enjoy the outdoors on holiday? Why do they go there?
g. Where do most people in you country go to relax at the weekend?
h. Do you think we should protect the natural environment? Why/ Why not?
i. Do most people in your country care about the environment? Why/ Why not?
j. How do people care for the environment in your country?
k. What kinds of pollution problems do you have in your country?
l. What kinds of natural disasters have you heard of? Give details.
m. What kinds of weather do you like best?

Focus on Part 2 of the IELTS Speaking Test

20 Read the prompt card below. What tense do you think you can use in your answer?

Describe a natural environment that you like (e.g. forest, lake, park, mountain).
You should say:
where it is
what you can see there
what people do there
and explain why you like this particular natural environment.

21 Listen to the candidate's long turn on this topic and answer the following questions.

a. What is the place and where is it?
b. What can you see there?
c. What animal did the candidate see one day?
d. What does the candidate say people do there?
e. Why does the candidate go there?
f. How does the candidate describe her feelings about the place? Give examples.

FLUENCY AND COHERENCE

22 Read the prompt card on the previous page again and choose a natural environment that you like.

23 Prepare for your long turn. Make quick notes. There are some extra prompts below to help you make your turn longer than one minute.

PROMPTS	YOUR NOTES
Where is it and what kind of place is it?	
How long does it take to get there? How do you get there?	
What can you see, hear or smell when you are there?	
Describe anything unusual about this place.	
Why do people go there and how often? What do people do there? Do they stay for a long time or just a few hours?	
Why do you like it?	

24 Now use your notes to tell your partner about the place you have chosen. Speak for ***more than one minute****. Ask your partner to time you.*

Partner: While you are listening and timing your partner, choose the most interesting points about the place they have chosen. After the talk, tell your partner what you were surprised about or interested in and why.

Script for Activity 9 — Student B (Student A uses questions from exercise 8)

Speaker 1

Our town is a beautiful historic city and a very international place but not overcrowded. There are lots of trees and nice people. The weather is very grey and gloomy in winter, but it's nice to live in beautiful Amsterdam, Netherlands.

Speaker 2

I live in an apartment in a big city. It's crowded, lots of traffic at all times of the day causing pollution. It's too hot most of the time. We have some beautiful beaches here in central Florida but I never get to them any more. I'd love to move. I'd go to the mountains any day.

Speaker 3

We have mountains and a beach nearby. The mountains are 15 minutes' drive away and the beach is 20 minutes' drive away. So people often drive to the mountains and spend the day walking, or go to the beach and enjoy swimming, although the beaches can become very crowded in the summer.

Speaker 4

In the heart of the city is a lake surrounded by a park with a cycling and walking track. The lake is clean and beautiful. Families often take picnics there and you can see people swimming, playing frisbee, rollerblading, all kinds of activities.

Speaker 5

Well, it's a sprawling suburban area with few stores or highways. There's not much industry and so the environment is not polluted. We get year round seasons, particularly a gorgeous fall. Unfortunately, the people keep to themselves most of the time and it's hard to make friends.

UNIT 9 Cooking and Special Occasions

Focus on Part 1 of the IELTS Speaking Test

WARM-UP

In the exam you may be asked questions about how to make your favourite dish.

Lin's boyfriend is coming for dinner. She decides to cook a Greek meal for him.

1 *Read the recipe below and use your dictionary to find the meaning of any words you don't know.*

Special Chicken

4 chicken thighs
2 tablespoons of lemon juice
1 or 2 cloves of crushed garlic
Salt & pepper
1½ tablespoons of oil
1 chopped onion
140g sour cream
100 ml chicken stock

1. Remove the skin from the chicken and marinate it overnight in lemon juice, garlic, salt and pepper.
2. Heat the oil in a frying pan.
3. Add the chopped onion and fry it until it is soft.
4. Add chicken pieces (with the marinade) and fry for 2 minutes until the outside of the chicken is brown.
5. Mix sour cream and chicken stock together and pour the mixture into the frying pan.
6. Cover with a lid and simmer for 45 minutes until the chicken is cooked.
7. Serve with rice and green vegetables.

VOCABULARY

2 *Work with a partner and ask each other questions about the ingredients in the recipe for Special Chicken. Remember to use 'How many' for countable nouns and 'How much' for uncountable nouns.*

For example:

How many chicken pieces do we need?

Four

How much lemon juice do we need?

2 tablespoons

Vocabulary Bank	
Nouns used in cooking	**Verbs used in cooking**
Ingredients	Remove
Recipe	Chop
Marinade	Pour
Bowl	Fry
Frying pan	Mix
Tablespoon	Heat
Cloves	Add
Sour cream	Stir
Thighs	Cover
Stock	Serve
Lid	Simmer
Juice	Marinate

3 *In the column on the left above, write each word in your own language.*

4 *Listen to the audio and repeat each word in the Vocabulary Bank. Concentrate on correct pronunciation.*

5 *Work with a partner. Read the following dialogue between the examiner and the candidate. The*

candidate uses three words in the answer to talk about the order in which the cake is put together. Find the three words.

Examiner: I'd like to ask you some questions about cooking. Can you tell me something about how to make your favourite dish?

Candidate: Oh yes. Well, one of my favourite recipes is for chocolate cake.

Examiner: What ingredients do you need to make a chocolate cake?

Candidate: I know you need some chocolate and flour and probably a few eggs, some sugar and some butter. I don't think you need any oil.

Examiner: And how do you make the cake? What do you do first?

Candidate: I don't spend much time cooking, so I don't remember exactly, but I think, **firstly**, you mix the butter and the sugar in a bowl and **then** add all the other ingredients and mix them all together. Of course, you don't add the egg shells! **Finally**, you put the cake into the oven and cook it.

Examiner: Who usually does the cooking in your house?
Candidate: In my family my parents share the cooking because my father is actually a very good cook and he enjoys cooking, so he cooks most weekdays and my mother cooks at the weekends.

6 *Underline all the ingredients of the chocolate cake in the dialogue above. Which of these underlined nouns are countable and which are uncountable?*

PRONUNCIATION

– s ending

	/ɪz/	/z/	/s/
Plural nouns	spice → spices /spaɪs/ → /spaɪsɪz/	onion → onions /ʌnjən/ → /ʌnjənz/	cake → cakes /keɪk/ → /keɪks/
3rd person	mix → mixes /mɪks/ → /mɪksɪz/	add → adds /æd/ → /ædz/	cook → cooks /kuk/ → kuks
Contractions of **is** and **has**		she is → she's / ʃɪ:/ → /ʃɪ:z/	it is → it's / ɪt/ → /ɪts/

/ɪz/ after /z/ /s/ /dz/ /tʃ/ /z/ /ʃ/
/z/ after any other voiced sound, including vowels
/s/ after any other voiceless sound

7 *How is the 's' ending pronounced in the following words? Write either /ɪz/ /z/ or /s/ after each word. The first one has been done for you.*

a.	Apples	/ z /	f.	He's	/ /
b.	Tomatoes	/ /	g.	Eggs	/ /
c.	Puts	/ /	h.	Cabbages	/ /
d.	Adds	/ /	i.	Cloves	/ /
e.	Vegetables	/ /	j.	Heats	/ /

8 *Listen to the audio and repeat each word being careful to pronounce the 's' ending correctly.*

9 *Read aloud the candidate's long turn above being careful to pronounce 's' endings correctly.*

GRAMMAR

Countable and Uncountable Nouns

Countable nouns can be singular and plural, e.g.: one onion, two onions.

Plural nouns usually end in 's', e.g.: There are four chicken thighs.

Uncountable nouns can only be singular, e.g.: There is some lemon juice.

Expressing Quantity with Countable and Uncountable Nouns

Countable and uncountable nouns are normally used with some in positive sentences and any in negative sentences or questions.

For example: *We have some oil and some onions.*

We don't have any onions.

Is there any chicken stock?

Countable nouns are used with **How many...?**

Uncountable nouns are used with **How much...?**

Much and many are also used with negatives and questions.

For example: *How much oil do we have?* *We don't have much oil.*

How many onions do we have? *We don't have many onions.*

A lot of or **lots of** is used with countable and uncountable nouns.

For example: *We have a lot of rice.* *Or : We have lots of rice.*

We have a lot of onions. *Or : We have lots of onions.*

A few is used with countable nouns.

A little is used with uncountable nouns.

For example: *There is a little oil.*

There are a few onions.

10 Add 's' to the countable nouns below. Do not add 's' to the uncountable nouns.

A few onion	A lot of oil	Some apple	Any flour
Many cabbage	A lot of egg	Some rice	Any butter

11 Fill in the gaps below using **some** *or* **any**.

a. You don't need ________oil, but you do need ___________ sour cream.
b. There are _____________ apples in the recipe.
c. Do you need _____________ lemon juice?
d. There aren't _____________ eggs in the recipe.

12 Fill in the gaps below using **much, many** *or* **a lot of**.

a. You have to cook ____________ rice.
b. How __________ chicken thighs do you need?
c. You don't need ______________oil.
d. How _____________ sour cream do you have?
e. There are ___________ onions in the recipe.

13 Check that **a few** *and* **a little** *are used correctly in the following sentences. Change the sentences that are incorrect. You may also need to change* **is** *and* **are**.

a. Do you need a few chicken stock?
b. I need a little butter.
c. There are a few oil in the recipe.
d. There is a little apples in the cake.
e. There are a few bananas and a lot of pineapples.

14 Work with a partner. One person is the examiner and the other the candidate. The candidate must talk about a favourite recipe or choose a recipe from the box below.

Recipes		
Stir fry chicken	Curry	Sweet & Sour Pork
Fried rice	Apple Cake	Pineapple cake

15 Take turns asking each other the following questions. Practise using different recipes. Remember, the examiner will be listening for the words **firstly**, **secondly**, **then**, **finally** *when you talk about how you make your recipe.*

Examiner: I'd like to ask you some questions about cooking. Can you tell me about one of your favourite recipes?

Candidate: Well, one of…

Examiner: What ingredients do you need to make ________________?

Candidate: I know you need…

Examiner: And how do you make ____________? What do you do first?

Candidate: I think you…

Examiner: Who usually does the cooking in your house?

Candidate: In my family…

Focus on Part 2 of the IELTS Speaking Test

16 *Write the names of some festivals or special days you have in your country. One has been done for you.*

17 *Talk about the types of food that you eat at these festivals or special days. Which is your favourite food? Why?*

18 *Read the following prompt card.*

> Describe a favourite dish that your family cooks for a special day or festival.
> You should say:
> what the dish is called
> which special day or festival it is cooked for
> how it is cooked
> and explain why it is a family favourite.

FLUENCY AND COHERENCE

19 *Read the following candidate's long turn. Choose words from the box below to fill in the gaps.*

When I was young, my mother used to make a cake every year for my birthday, ____________now I am older she always cooks my favourite meal, which is curry.

The ingredients for curry are a little______, onions, garlic, _______ meat, tinned tomatoes, chilli and curry spices. My mother doesn't buy _______ curry powder from the supermarket, ______ __________she makes it herself.

First, she __________the oil in a pan and adds the chopped onions and crushed garlic _____________. Then she adds the meat and __________ it until it is brown. After that she puts in all her curry spices. I like curry hot so she _______ a lot of chilli. Finally, she adds the tomatoes and stirs it all.

She cooks it with a lid on for about one hour and serves it with rice and_______________.

I love curry because the taste is so delicious and spicy. It has lots of flavour.

Oil	but instead	whereas	fries	some
adds	any	heats	cloves	vegetables

20 Listen to the audio of the candidate's long turn and check whether you are correct.

*21 Underline the words the candidate uses to talk about the order in which their mother makes the curry, for example, '**first**'.*

Contrasting

22 In the following paragraph, find and underline two words or phrases used for contrasting two facts.

When I was young, my mother used to make a cake every year for my birthday, whereas now I am older, she always cooks my favourite meal, which is curry. The ingredients for curry are a little oil, onions, garlic, some meat, tinned tomatoes, chilli and curry spices. My mother doesn't buy any curry powder from the supermarket, but instead she makes it herself.

Contrasting conjunctions:
but is the most common word in English for contrasting two facts.
whereas is also used to contrast two facts. It is more formal than **but**.
but instead is used to talk about in the place of. You choose to do another thing rather than the first thing.

23 Work with a partner.

Student A reads Card A and Student B reads Card B on the next page.
Card B is not in the correct order.
Find the correct phrases to complete Student A's sentences.

For example:

When I was young, I liked sweet food _______ now I prefer savoury food.

*Then join the sentences together using **but**, **whereas** or **but instead**.*

For example:

When I was young, I liked sweet food whereas now I prefer savoury food.

Note: In some sentences all three contrasting words can be used, but not in every sentence.

CARD A		CARD B
1. When I was young, I liked sweet food...		___________my sister likes sweet food.
2. My Dad used to eat too much...		___________ now I cook once or twice a week.
3. I like hot, spicy food...		___________now I prefer savoury food.
4. We usually eat at 6 pm...		___________Rob's brother eats a lot and gets fat.
5. Rob eats a lot and stays thin...		___________now he is dieting.
6. When I was young, I never cooked...		___________recently we've eaten at 7 pm.

24 *With a partner, make your own contrasting sentences using the following ideas. Use the words **but**, **whereas** or **but instead**.*

a. When I was young...
b. I like to eat fast food...
c. My friend likes...
d. My mother wanted Chicken Stir Fry...

25 *Read again the prompt card for 'Cooking' and choose your own favourite recipe for a festival or special day. You have one minute to make notes. Use what you learnt in this unit to help you.*

Recipe name	
Which festival?	
How to cook	
Firstly....	
Why favourite?	

26 *In pairs, listen to each other's long turn. Try to speak for at least one minute.*

UNIT 10 Transport

Focus on Part 1 of the IELTS Speaking Test

WARM-UP

1 Listen to the statements about transport and tick the boxes which show which forms of transport the speakers talk about. The first one has been done for you.

SPEAKER 1	walk √	bicycle	car √	bus	. train	boat	plane
SPEAKER 2	walk	bicycle	car	bus	train	boat	plane
SPEAKER 3	walk	bicycle	car	bus	train	boat	plane
SPEAKER 4	walk	bicycle	car	bus	train	boat	plane
SPEAKER 5	walk	bicycle	car	bus	train	boat	plane
SPEAKER 6	walk	bicycle	car	bus	train	boat	plane
SPEAKER 7	walk	bicycle	car	bus	train	boat	plane

2 Listen to the statements again. For each, write the full statements in the boxes below as you hear them. Then count how many words are used and write the number in the spaces below (contractions like 'don't' should be counted as two words). The first one has been done for you.

	Full Statements	Words
SPEAKER 1	No, I don't have a car, so I walk to work everyday.	13
SPEAKER 2		
SPEAKER 3		
SPEAKER 4		
SPEAKER 5		
SPEAKER 6		
SPEAKER 7		

VOCABULARY

Vocabulary Bank

Nouns and noun phrases	Verbs
public transport transportation traffic jams problems rush hour gasoline petrol tax high-rise parking buildings penalty cycle lane / bike lane speed limit journey suburb commuters delay motorway	to break down to increase to decrease to hit to delay to roll about / roll around to cycle/bike

You can travel by ...	Trains and buses can be ...	Journeys can be ...	A transportation problem may include ...
commuter train	cramped	bumpy	a breakdown
ferry	crowded	eventful	a cancellation of service
monorail	draughty	nerve-racking	congested roads
motorcycle	jam-packed	relaxing	a delayed service
scooter	shabby	tedious	a detour
subway	stuffy	tiring	erratic driving
taxi	convenient	frustrating	a hold-up
tube	expensive		roadworks
underground train	efficient		a traffic diversion
bicycle	comfortable		a traffic jam
on foot	uncomfortable		

3 Use your dictionary to find the meaning of any words you don't know.

4 Listen to the words on the audio and repeat.

PRONUNCIATION

In natural spoken English words are linked together.

A word that begins with a vowel is linked to the last consonant sound (or vowel sound, in some cases) of the word before it.

For example: Speaker 1 says: 'I don't **have a** car...'

'**have**' is linked to '**a**', since the last sound in 'have' is a consonant /v/ and the first sound in 'a' is a vowel sound /ə/.

5 *Listen to the statements on the audio again and underline the words that are linked (as in Speaker 1 example on the first page of this unit).*

6 *Practise saying the sentences linking the words together.*

7 *Read the Part 1 questions below. Match them to the answers in Exercise 1 of the Warm-up section above. The first one has been done for you.*

a. What kinds of transport do you use everyday when you are in your country? = Speaker 2
b. How far do you travel every day?
c. What transport do you use most often? Why?
d. How do you get to school every day?
e. What form of transport do you prefer? Why?
f. Do you live near your school?
g. Do you drive to work?

8 *Now underline the links in the questions as shown in example (a) above.*

9 *Take turns asking and answering the questions with your partner. Remember to link the underlined words.*

10 *Ask the questions again, but this time answer them in your own words speaking about what you do.*

GRAMMAR

In Part 1, you may be asked about the kinds of transport you use everyday. It is important to speak naturally, which includes giving added information—as long as it is relevant. Notice how the speaker uses conjunctions ***because*** and ***but*** to extend the answer:

'I usually go to work by train ***because*** it's convenient, ***but*** sometimes I walk for the exercise.'

Other common conjunctions are ***and***, ***so***, ***or***, and ***then***.

Conjunction	Meaning	Example
because	the reason why	I usually go to work by train because it's convenient.
but	in contrast	I usually go to work by train, but sometimes I walk.
and	in addition	I travel 27 kilometres by bus and 3 kilometres by boat everyday.
so	the result of (fact 2 is the result of fact 1)	No, I don't have a car, so I walk to work everyday.
or	another way/alternative	I use a bicycle or I walk to school.
then	one thing happens after another	I walk to the bus stop. Then I get on the bus.

Put it all together

11 Listen to Part 1 of a sample interview. Which questions from Exercise 1 did the interviewer ask?

*12 Take turns with your partner asking the questions again in Exercise 7 above. To answer, speak about what **you** do. This time extend your answers giving more information by using the common conjunctions in the table above.*

Focus on Part 2 of the IELTS Speaking Test

13 Work with your partner to brainstorm the topic of 'Transportation Problems'.

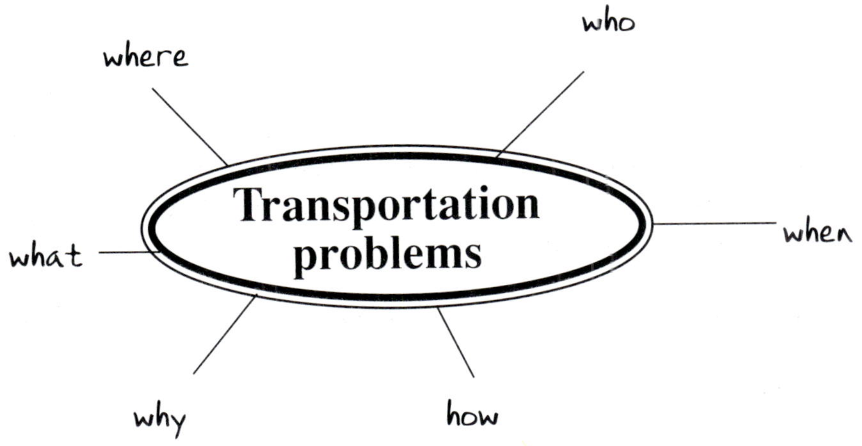

14 Look at this note:

'too many old cars'

See how it is extended:

'There are too many old cars, which break down often and cause traffic problems'.

Transform each note below into longer statements:

a. 'parking spaces too far from shops'
b. 'not enough trains'
c. 'buses don't run on time'
d. 'traffic jams at rush hour'
e. 'gasoline is too expensive'
f. 'cars go too fast'

15 With your partner, take turns asking and answering:

'What problems are there with transport in your city?'

16 Read the following two prompt cards.

Listen to the long turn. Which prompt card is this candidate talking about, A or B?

A Describe the public transport system in your city.
You should say:
  what kinds of transport there are
  how efficient the different transport systems are
  what kind of transport you use
and explain why you choose to use this form of transportation.

B Describe a journey you make every day.
You should say:
  where you travel to and from
  how long it takes
  what kind of transport you use
and explain why you choose this form of transportation.

17 Read the transcript of the long turn and underline the conjunctions that are used to extend the answers.

On weekdays, and sometimes on the weekend, I go to the university in the city from my house in Ranui, which is in a Western suburb. It's quite far, about 30 kilometres, and it takes an hour, but I don't mind the journey because I do all the reading for my university on the train.

Every morning I get up at 6 o'clock. I have to get up this early to get to university on time, if I go by train. So I get up at 6 o'clock and I have to leave the house by ten to seven to get the 7.15 train. It only takes about 15 minutes to walk to the train station, but I leave myself plenty of time because the trains are never on time! Often they're late, but sometimes they are early! A couple of times last year they never came and I had to wait over an hour! The trains are quite old so they often break down.

This is another reason why I need to get to the station early—in case I have to get a bus. If the train breaks down, you see, the train company is supposed to send buses for the commuters, but when this happens it takes much longer to get to the city because of the delay and because the bus stops many times along the way. So that's why I have to leave early! If there is a breakdown, I usually get to university late for my lecture, even if I leave home early. It's rather frustrating!

But I do prefer taking the train because you can read or write on board, even use a laptop! Buses, on the other hand, are very uncomfortable. They make you roll about as they move and when they stop, you have to stop writing or else you make a big mess on your paper! The last time I took a bus I gave up trying to write after ten minutes! I have been thinking about riding a bicycle to the city recently. It's a very long journey though, but it would be good for exercise! There is a bike lane along the motorway now, so it is much safer than it used to be and I wouldn't have to leave home any earlier in the morning than I do now, since cycling is quite fast.

I think I will end up cycling to university...maybe after my exams. It would be a much nicer journey I think.

FLUENCY AND COHERENCE

18 Using prompt card A above make your own notes ready for your long turn. Speak for at least one minute. Extend your long turn by using conjunctions.

In the IELTS test you will only have one minute to prepare, but for this unit you may take longer so that you can think about extending your answer by using conjunctions wherever possible. Use the prompts to help you.

Prompts	Your Notes
Kinds of transport in your city *(Give as many examples as you can.)*	
Most efficient kinds of transport *(Can you give more than one example? Extend your answer with reasons.)*	
Less efficient kinds of transport *(Give more than one example if possible and extend your answer with reasons.)*	
Transport you use *(To extend your answer, think about whether you have always used this transport or whether you generally use more than one kind.)*	
Why you choose this transport *(To extend, think about a personal story, or, if you have changed transport, give reasons.)*	

19 Use the topic card below to practise another long turn. Take time to make notes first. Think about how you can give more information for each prompt. As you listen to your partner, count the number of times that he or she uses the conjunctions ***because****,* ***but****,* ***so****, or* ***then****.*

Describe the kind of transport you use most often.
You should say:
what it is
when you use it
what you like about it
and explain what problems there are with it.

Focus on Part 3 of the IELTS Speaking Test

In Part 3 of the test, you are frequently asked to offer solutions to problems. One way of doing this is to use the **First Conditional**.

If + **present** tense, **will** + **base form** of the verb.

For example:

Problem — There are too many old cars which break down and cause traffic jams.
Solution — Government tax

Using the first conditional, this answer can be extended to:
'**If** the government **puts** a tax on old cars, there **will be** fewer breakdowns and traffic jams.'

20 *Using the first conditional, give extended answers for each solution to the problems below.*

Problem	Solution
There is not enough parking near the shopping centre. Many cyclists are hit by cars. There are too many high speed crashes.	construct high-rise parking buildings make special cycle lanes; lower the speed limit

21 *Think of your own solutions to the following problems and give extended answers using the first conditional.*

Problem	Solution
The buses don't run on time. People don't use public transport. Some taxi drivers are bad drivers. Old vehicles make a lot of air pollution. There is too much traffic noise in the city centre.	… … … … …

22 *Practise with a partner. Student A states a problem from either of the two tables above. Student B gives a solution (with a first conditional).*

For example:

A – 'There are too many high speed crashes.'
B – 'If the Government lowers the speed limit, there will be fewer high speed accidents.'

Speaking

UNIT 11 News Sources

Focus on Part 1 of the IELTS Speaking Test

WARM-UP

1 *What is news? What is opinion? Are these all news stories? Do you agree with your partner?*

a. Bush will send more US soldiers to Iraq.
b. My IELTS teacher has a terrible hairstyle.
c. Chocolate is too sweet.
d. Chinese astronaut walks in space.
e. 10 reasons why you should buy a new computer this year.
f. New Zealand signs trade deal with China.

News Sources

2 *Where do you get the best news and information about your family? From your mother, your father, or from another source? Where do you get news about your country or region or the world? Answer for yourself and put a tick or a cross in the following table.*

	News about			
SOURCE	1.Your family	SOURCE	2.Your country	3.The world
grandparents?		local newspapers?		
parents?		friends?		
brother/sister?		local TV/radio?		
uncles/aunts?		the Internet?		
friends?		family?		
other?		other?		

3 Now take turns asking and answering with your partner. Use the survey form above and fill in the boxes about your ***partner*** *this time.*

For example:

A: Do you get any news about… e.g. your family…from… e.g. your uncle or aunt?

B: Yes, I do. / No, I don't.
I get some/a lot of /a little /no news about…from my…

VOCABULARY

Synonyms are words or phrases that have the same meaning.

4 Underline the synonyms in each sentence.

For example:

My school **doesn't allow** chewing gum. It is not **permitted**.

a. My parents screened all my phone calls, and censored all my emails.
b. When my dad turned 50, he kept the news under wraps, in a veil of secrecy.
c. The city bans the consumption of alcohol in public places, and prohibits loud noise after 10pm.
d. After 9/11, there was a blackout of information from the US media—all news was suppressed.

Vocabulary Bank

Noun	Adjective	Collocations
ban	condemned	a regulatory body
deception	controversial	at the discretion of
disclosure	critical	in confidence
discretion	crucial	on moral grounds
moral	devious	to be deceptive about sth.
principle	discerning	to conceal (something)
regulation	discriminating	to filter
	hard-hitting	to keep a secret
	prohibited	to keep under wraps
	provocative	to regulate (something)
	righteous	to screen for (something)
	significant	to suppress information
	thought-provoking	to withhold information

PRONUNCIATION

Sentence Stress

5 *Listen to the audio. Which words are stressed in the following sentence?*

Do you get any news about your region from the Internet?

The words **news**, **your region**, and **Internet** are louder than the others.
This is because in English words that carry the most meaning are stressed, and words that carry less meaning are not stressed.
We usually stress negative words. e.g. **can't**, **don't**, **won't**, **not**, **no**.

• • ● ● • • • ● • • • ●

E.g. I get no news about my region from my friends.

6 *Listen to the audio and put the sentences below into the boxes that match their different stress patterns. Some sentences have the same pattern. One has been done for you.*

I hate computers!	Turn to page nine.	I don't agree.
Keep quiet!	What's happening?	It's very funny!
It's full of good news.	It's there!	Read the paper.
Don't waste time.	Don't forget!	What do you know?
He bought it.	Keep up!	I haven't seen it.
It's in the news.	Tell us the news.	Not now!
One.	I agree.	Come and look!

●	•●	● ●	● ●•
••●	•●•	●•●	●•●•
•●•●	●••●	•● •●• I hate computers!	•●•●●

7 *Now listen again and repeat with the correct sentence stress.*

GRAMMAR

Present perfect

We use the present perfect to show that an action, which happened in the past, still has a connection with the present.

Form: have + past participle

Examples 1 of present perfect use:

Talking about our experience up to now in our life, i.e. from birth to now:

- Have you ever read a newspaper from start to finish? Yes, I have.
- Have you ever bought a magazine? Yes, I have. I bought my first magazine when I was a teenager.

→ If the time period is important, i.e. we want to say '**when**', we have to use the past simple tense, e.g.: I bought my first magazine when I was a teenager.

8 *Answer the following typical Part 1 questions. Remember to add one piece of extra information to your yes/no answer.*

Have you ever read a foreign newspaper?
Have you ever met a famous person?

Example 2 of present perfect use:

Uncompleted action that began in the past and continues in the present where we can still see the results:

- How long have you lived in your city? I've lived there for 5 years—since my family moved from the countryside.

9 *Write the questions for these answers. Use the present perfect.*

a. ____?

It's been an international newspaper for 20 years.

b. ____?

I've bought that magazine every week since 2001.

Example 3 of present perfect use:

Describing present result of past action or change:

- Newspapers have changed. There is much more international news now.

Example 4 of present perfect use:

Describing something that has just happened recently:

- I'm sorry the magazine has just been sold out.

In newspaper headlines, the present perfect is often suggested (although the present simple is used):

New Zealand signs trade deal with China.

The meaning is → NZ has just/recently signed the trade deal.

US forces captured Saddam Hussein.

The meaning is → US troops have just/recently captured him.

10 Write the present perfect meaning under each of the headlines below:

I. Earthquake Hits New York
II. IELTS Exam Cancelled
III. Latest Model Mobile Phone Released
IV. Olympic Games Start!
V. Twenty-two Baby Alligators Found in New York Sewers

You may be asked a present perfect question in the IELTS Speaking Test. Make sure you answer with the present perfect too.

11 Make questions from the words below using the present perfect.

For example:

ever watch/English movie?
Have you ever watched an English movie?

a. ever read / English newspaper?
b. ever buy / teenager's magazine?
c. parents / ever stop / you watching TV program?
d. How long / own / mobile phone?

12 Work with your partner. Ask and answer the questions above. Add more information to your answer, and don't just say one word.

If you add extra information about '**when** something happened', use the **past simple**.
If you add information about '**how long for**', use the **present perfect** and '**since**'.

Focus on Part 2 of the IELTS Speaking Test

13 Ask and answer with your partner:

- What TV programs did you enjoy watching when you were a child? Which ones were you allowed/not allowed to watch when you were 10 years old?
- What magazines do you read now? Which ones were you allowed/not allowed to read when you were 10 years old?

Cause and effect

Giving reasons for your answers is a natural way of extending your presentation in Part 2 of the IELTS speaking test.

14 Match the cause or reason on the left with the effect or result on the right. The first one has been done for you.

REASON	Answer	RESULT
a. She's embarrassed by what happened.	F	A. My phone number is unlisted.
b. The TV program was full of violent images.		B. People talk about what's happening in other countries.
c. I can see familiar places.		C. Nobody bought it.
d. I'm worried about security.		D. It has an R16 censor's rating.
e. My parents were concerned about explicit content.		E. I like local TV.
f. There's more international news now.		F. Nobody talks about it.
g. The newspaper had boring stories.		G. It was only shown late at night.
h. This movie is for adults.		H. We weren't allowed to surf the Internet.

15 Work with a partner to join your sentences using the following words or phrases to make reason/result or result/reason sentences. Then listen to check your answers.

Reason + so + RESULT

For example:

The TV programs contained bad language and violence, so our parents censored them.

RESULT + because + Reason

For example:

Our parents censored the TV programs because of the bad language and violence.

FLUENCY AND COHERENCE

Describe your favourite news source.
You should say:

- how often you use this news source
- why you use this source
- what other sources you use

and how you would change that news source if you could.

16 Listen to and read the Part 2 long turn on the above topic. Note the following strategies the candidate uses.

I. First, highlight where the candidate supports his statements with reasons. The first one has been done for you.
II. Then underline the words he uses to express his feelings.
III. Circle where he refers to a past situation.
IV. Mark where he uses examples from his own life in answering the question.

These are strategies that are usually successful in helping to create a natural-sounding response to a Part 2 question.

My favourite source of news is the student radio station in Auckland. I get news from this station almost every day, depending on whether or not I do much driving, **because the radio is in my car**. It has really funny hosts, so I like it a lot. Sometimes the news items or the way they are read is <u>so funny, it makes me really laugh</u>. But the news items are always interesting, and informative. And I like the way they don't censor their feelings—they often laugh or give strong opinions over the radio.

The reports of events are often quite well analyzed, from many different points of view, so they are a good source of news and entertainment. I've been listening to them for years! Another reason why I get news from this station is because they play the best music, compared with all the other stations. I used to listen to the National Radio station for news, and they also have intelligent commentaries, but not as good music! I prefer radio as a way of getting news because I don't have time to read a newspaper, and anyway, the only daily newspaper in this city is very boring—full of crime stories and sport! Sometimes, I get news from the Internet but usually by accident, as I log on to my email account. I do read the local papers, however, because they have important information about this community and at least one in particular doesn't have sensational crime stories. There are articles in it about upcoming events here and sometimes useful information that helps you get by—like sales or bargains, or a story about the area from someone who has lived here a long time. I saw my photo in this paper a few weeks ago! I would like the paper to have less advertising, however. It makes it too hard to find the interesting parts!

17 Read the prompt card below and make notes for each of the points.

Describe your favourite magazine or newspaper.
You should say:
- where you usually buy it
- what parts of it you most enjoy reading
- where you usually read it

and say how it compares to other things you read.

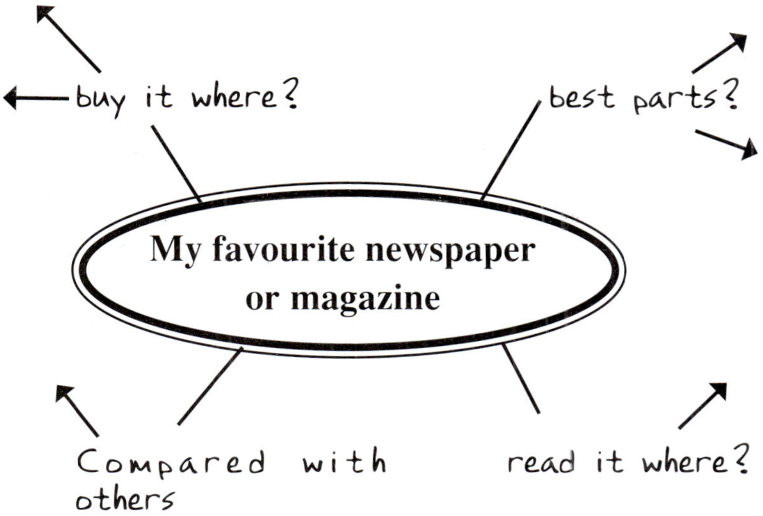

18 Now take turns timing yourself and your partner using your notes to speak for at least one and a half minutes describing your favourite magazine or newspaper. Be sure to use the strategies mentioned in this lesson:

Strategies:

- Can I give a reason?
- What's an example from my life?
- I'm allowed to say how I feel/felt.
- Can I add information to this?
- Relax and keep friendly eye-contact!
- Can I compare with what I used to do?

Speaking

UNIT 12 Leisure Activities

Focus on Part 1 of the IELTS Speaking Test

WARM-UP

1 Listen to these Part 1 sentences and repeat.

a. In my free time, I always text my friends.
b. One of my hobbies is taking photos of my friends and putting them on Facebook.
c. Playing computer games is one of my favourite things to do.
d. I like to relax by reading gossip about celebrities online.
e. When I'm not studying, I like to sleep! I love taking naps.

VOCABULARY

Vocabulary Bank

Hobbies can be...	Outdoor pastimes	Indoor pastimes
beneficial	bird watching	art and craft
challenging	countryside walks	board games
energetic	fishing	chess
enthralling	gardening	coin collecting
fascinating	painting	computer games
intriguing	photography	embroidery
monotonous	shopping	entertaining
popular	star-gazing	knitting
relaxing		listening to music
satisfying		modelling
tranquil		movies
		patchwork quilting
		scrapbooking
		sewing
		stamp collecting

2 *Look at the leisure time activities in the boxes. Tick ✓ the activities which you like doing.*

playing computer games	looking at websites	chatting on MSN or QQ	going to the cinema	eating out
reading novels	taking photos	texting friends	sleeping	spending time with friends
listening to music	talking on the phone	going out for coffee	playing PS3	reading magazines
watching DVDs		karaoke	shopping at the mall with friends	

3 *Name the activities below.*

A

B

C

D

E

F

4 *What other leisure activities do you enjoy which are not in the box above?*

______________________ ______________________

______________________ ______________________

5 *Look at the following dialogue from Part 1 of the speaking test. Match the examiner's questions with the candidate's answers.*

EXAMINER

A
Hello, my name's Mary—what's your full name please?

CANDIDATE

I
Yes, I do think that people probably should have more free time nowadays, because life is so much busier and more stressful that we need more time to relax.

B
Okay Charlie. Could I see your identification please?

C
Okay. For the first part of the test, I'd like to talk to you about free time. How much free time do you have?

D
Do you think people these days should have more free time?

II
My full name's Ling Bo, but you can call me Charlie.

III
Sure. Here you are.

IV
What do you usually do in your free time?

V
Apart from studying, I like to chat with my friends online for fun and I also love going to the movies to relax.

VI
I'm studying quite hard at the moment, so I don't have a lot of free time!

6 *Listen to the audio and check your answers.*

PRONUNCIATION

7 *Listen again and underline the words in the candidate's answers which are stressed.*

For example:

My **full** name is **Ling Bo**, but you can call me **Char**lie.
Da **DA** da da **DA DA** da da da da da DA da

8 *Repeat the candidate's answers focusing on the sentence stress.*

9 *Now fill in the answers to the questions with information about yourself.*

a. My full name is ____________________ but you can call me ______________.
b. Sure, here you are.
c. I am ____________________ at the moment, so I ____ ____________.
d. I like to ______________________________ and I also love ______________________________ _____once in a while.
e. I think that people______________________________because ____________________________ ______________________________.

10 *Mark the stressed words in your answers and practise saying them aloud.*

GRAMMAR

Adverbial phrases can tell us a lot about how often we do something, as you learned in Unit 3, but they can also express why we do something: purpose. Look at these sentences from the Part 1 Speaking interview.

I like to chat with my friends online **for fun**.
I also love going to the movies **to relax**.

11 Look at the following adverbial phrases. Can you divide them into two groups? Which grammatical pattern do you notice?

to relax	to spend time with my friends	for fun
for enjoyment	to enjoy myself	to have fun
to be creative	for entertainment	to buy stuff
to get good marks	to socialise with my classmates	
to practise my English	to meet new people	
for communication	to communicate with my friends	
to keep in touch with friends overseas		

12 Listen to these sentences from the Part 1 Speaking interview. Repeat the sentences.

I like to chat with my friends online **for fun**.
I also love going to the movies **to relax**.

13 Listen and repeat the following sentences paying special attention to the stress pattern of the sentence.

a. I like to take photos for fun.
b. I use Facebook to keep in touch with my friends.
c. I read novels in my spare time for relaxation.
d. I study English in my free time to get good marks.
e. I play computer games to have fun.

14 Write five sentences about what you like to do in your leisure time. Use an adverbial phrase with each sentence to say why you like doing the activity.

a. ______________________________

b. ______________________________

c. ______________________________

d. ______________________________

e. ______________________________

15 *Say each sentence aloud to your partner, paying attention to the stress pattern.*

Put it all together

16 *Roleplay*

Student A: *You are the examiner. Ask your partner the Part 1 questions in Activity 5 above.*

Student B: *You are the IELTS candidate. Answer the questions speaking about yourself.*

Now swap roles: Student A, you are the candidate. Student B, you are the examiner.

TIP
These roleplays will help you feel more comfortable in knowing what to expect on the day of the test. Try it!

Focus on Part 2 of the IELTS Speaking Test

17 *Look at the following Part 2 prompt card and the notes which the candidate has made. Can you predict what they will speak about by looking at their notes?*

Describe your favourite leisure activity.
You should say:
what you do
when and where you do it
whether you do it alone or with other people
and explain why you enjoy this leisure activity.

18 *The prompt card has four questions/sections. Read a candidate's long turn, which is a little mixed up. Can you find the four sections of the candidate's long turn?*

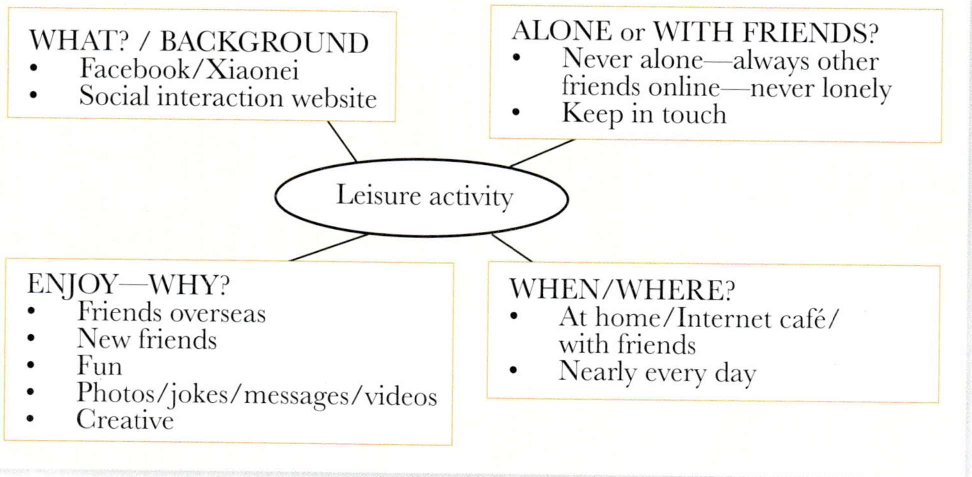

'You are never alone on sites like Facebook and Xiaonei, because of the way they work. So I guess this is a type of leisure activity which I'm always doing with friends, whether I am actually with them or not! It is so popular with me and my friends, and I think it will just get more popular in the future. Well, I guess one of my favourite leisure activities is posting on Xiaonei, which is a Chinese website. Actually, it's really similar to Facebook, but it was started by a couple of Chinese university students. You can invite people to be your 'friends' and then you can chat with them, and share all sorts of stuff: photos, music, videos, gossip, join groups…anything really! I like Xiaonei because I can keep up with what all my friends are up to, and it doesn't matter if they are in Shanghai or Sydney, so it's a really good way to keep in touch. The other reason I like it is that you don't have to send a long email to keep in touch, you can just send someone a smiley face or whatever to let them know you are thinking about them. And the photo feature is great. I mean you get to see all these photos of your friends and you don't have to wait ages for them to download as an attachment. And you can set up your own page to be quite personal, which I like, because you can be a bit creative. And you can use it anywhere, well anywhere where you have the Internet. So I use it at home on my laptop, or at an Internet café, and yeah, I probably use it almost every day, I would say. I'm getting addicted to it!'

Colloquial or informal language

19 *Look at the following colloquial language from the tapescript. Match each word or expression to its definition on the right. Read the sentence in the tapescript where these words are found and try to guess the meaning before you use a dictionary.*

up to	to wait for a long time
keep in touch	doing
set up	stay in contact with someone
to wait ages	create/start
whatever	lots of people like it
popular	any or everything
stuff	things

20 *Ask and answer the following questions with your partner.*

a. How do you keep in touch with your friends?
b. When was the last time you had to wait ages for something?
c. What is the most popular leisure activity among you and your friends?
d. What were you up to at this time yesterday?

*21 Now it is your turn. Make notes about the same prompt card: '**Describe your favourite leisure activity**'. Make good use of your preparation time. Your notes will help you to structure your talk and give you confidence.*

WHAT is it?

____
____
____

WHEN & WHERE do you do it?

____
____
____

WHY do you enjoy it?

____
____
____

WHO do you do it with?

____
____
____

22 Begin your long turn using your notes to help you. Speak for at least one minute. Try to go for two minutes, if possible. Get your partner to time you.

Focus on Part 3 of the IELTS Speaking Test

In Part 3 of the IELTS speaking test, the examiner will ask you more abstract questions connected to the Part 2 topic. You may be asked to compare the past with the present or the present with the future.

For example:

How have the types of leisure activities changed in your country over the last fifty years?

23 Write your ideas below in short notes.

Leisure activities in the past	Leisure activities now

24 With your partner, ask and answer the question using your notes above. Be sure to include words that show 'contrast'.

However; whereas; while; but; but instead

For example:

People used to play mah-jong. **However**, nowadays they are more likely to use the Internet to play games.

I think children's leisure activities have changed a lot over the years. They used to play outside more often **whereas** now they spend hours inside in front of the television.

Here is another typical Part 3 question:

Why do you think the older generation enjoy different leisure activities to the younger generation?

*25 With your partner, ask and answer the question above. This time include **introductory phrases** and '**reason/result**' or '**result/reason**' sentence structures.*

Introductory phrases:

In my opinion...
It seems to me that...
Well, I think...
I think one of the reasons...

Reason = **because**; Result = **so**

For example:

I think one of the reasons is that the older generation have less energy than the younger generation, **so** they need less energetic leisure activities.

In my opinion the younger generation prefer to use technology in their free time **because** they grew up in a different era to the older generation.

UNIT 13 Technology and Equipment

Focus on Part 1 of the IELTS Speaking Test

WARM-UP

1 *Look at the following aspects of life. How have they been made easier by technology? Discuss some examples with a partner.*

education housework shopping communication entertainment work transport diet

2 *Now think ahead to the year 2040. Brainstorm each topic and think about how life might be different in this area. Write at least 2 things for each topic below in the note form. The first one has been done for you.*

housework: automatic vacuum cleaners, remote control dish washers

entertainment:

studying:

shopping:

communication:

work:

transport:

diet:

3 *Listen to the following speakers discussing life in 2040. Write the topic from above which the speaker mentions. The first one has been done for you.*

Speaker1: ___Transport___

Speaker 2: ________

Speaker 3: ________

Speaker 4: ________

Speaker 5: ________

VOCABULARY

4 *Underline the vocabulary in each script which helped you to decide which topic the speakers were discussing.*

Speaker 1: I think people could definitely fly around in little cars which'll be like personal mini-aeroplanes. It'll be so much faster and better than sitting in traffic!

Speaker 2: Well, I'm sure I won't have to go to school anymore! Everything will be done over the Internet in virtual classrooms. And hopefully it'll be so much easier to learn a new language.

Speaker 3: There'll probably be lots more online computer games which players and friends all over the world can join. And if I have a friend in Sydney, I'll be able to go virtual shopping with her!

Speaker 4: You might be able to download movies and songs to a chip which you insert in your brain!

Speaker 5: We may just take a pill instead of eating real food. Not as enjoyable but perhaps it means there'll be enough food for everyone.

Vocabulary Bank

Communication Item	Personal Item	Household Item
iPod	digital camera	picture / web frame
personal data access (PDA)	mp3	scales
global positioning system (GPS)	laptop	microwave
cordless phone	notebook	oven
cell / mobile phone	info pad (for the elderly)	clothes dryer
Internet		dishwasher
web camt		washing machine
		security system
		DVD player

5 *Look at the following items of technology on the left and match them with their functions and definitions on the right. The first one has been done for you.*

Mobile phone/cell phone	Like an MP3 player, also stores photos and other stuff
Dishwasher	A machine which cleans dirty clothes
DVD player	A small, portable, music playing device
Laptop	A phone you can take anywhere
PC	This plays movies at home on your TV
Digital camera	Takes digital images
Playstation 3	A portable computer
Blackberry	A desktop computer
MP3 player	A machine which cleans dirty dishes
Washing machine	Video game console
Ipod	A handheld device, also called a smartphone, which can send and receive emails

6 *Listen and mark the stress in each word, e.g. cell phone.*

7 *Listen again and repeat each word.*

8 *Make a list of ten items of technology that are important to you, your family and your friends. You can use ideas from the previous activity.*

9 *Rank how important each item is to you personally, from 1 (the most important) to 10 (the least important). Compare your answers with a partner.*

10 *Choose your three most important technological possessions and complete the table below.*

Piece of equipment	Function: What does it do?	Adjectives	Why you like it...
E.g. mobile phone	call text games photos	great convenient cheap tiny	Because I can text my friends and always stay in contact.

PRONUNCIATION

11 When speaking, it is more natural to use contractions. Listen to speaker 2 from activity 3 again:

'Well, I'm sure I won't have to go to school anymore! Everything will be done over the Internet in virtual classrooms. And hopefully it'll be so much easier to learn a new language.'

12 Listen and repeat the contracted forms of will.

I'll	**We'll**
It'll	**There'll**
Won't	**You'll**

13 Listen and repeat.

a. **It'll** be so much easier to learn a new language.
b. **There'll** be enough food for everyone.
c. **I'll** be able to go virtual shopping with my friend in Sydney.
d. **I won't** have to go to school anymore.
e. **You'll be** able to fly around in your own personal aeroplane.

GRAMMAR

14 Look at the script in activity 4. Which auxiliary verbs or adverbs have the speakers used to talk about the future? Write them in the box. The first two have been done for you.

Will	________________	________________
Will probably	________________	________________

*15 Order the modal verbs from 1 (**not likely to happen**) to 5 (**very likely to happen**). 'Will' has been done for you.*

1 ——————————————————————————→ 5

will

When making predictions about the future, you can use the modal verbs in the box above together with a base verb. Look at this sentence from the listening task:

'There **will** probably **be** lots more online computer games.'

Different modal verbs express different degrees of probability, or the likelihood of something occurring. The adverbs ***probably*** and ***definitely*** change position in the sentence depending on whether the sentence is positive or negative.

For example:

Mandarin **will probably** be the most popular language.
English **probably won't** be useful anymore!
I **will definitely** pass the IELTS test.
I **definitely won't** be at school.

16 Now write your own predictions about 2040, or further into the future if you prefer.

a. (use **will and definitely**)

____

b. (use **might**)

____

c. (use **may**)

____

d. (use **will not and probably**)

____

e. (use **will be able to**)

____

f. (use **could**)

____

FLUENCY AND COHERENCE

In the IELTS Speaking Exam, the examiner will be listening to how fluently you speak English, that is, whether you can keep speaking without long pauses.

17 *Read the prompt card below and choose one item from your own technological possessions to talk about. Using your notes, prepare for your long turn. Try to talk for two minutes. You may find the language in the bubbles after the task card helpful:*

> Describe a piece of technological equipment that you own and like.
> You should say:
>   what it is
>   what you use it for
>   how it is useful
> and explain why you like it.

18 *Look at the following Part 2 topic card. How is the tense different to what you have just talked about?*

> Describe a piece of equipment that you would like to own.
> You should say:
>   what it is
>   what it is useful for
>   how or when you would use it
> and explain why you want to have it.

TIP

Look at the tense on the topic card: you are being asked to speak about something you do ***not*** own, but ***would like to have***. Because you are imagining, you can use ***would*** and ***could*** to speculate about what it would be like to own this piece of equipment.

19 Listen to the speaker discussing this topic. Can you guess what he is talking about? How?

'Okay...I would really love to own a ***** I think they are amazing, because they are so tiny, and they can do so many things! I really like the way they look—so slim and light. But the incredible thing is what they can do. A ***** is kind of three things in one—a phone, an iPod and a computer. So it is really useful, because you can do all the things you normally do with a phone, like texting and calling people, but you can also listen to your favourite music and surf the net. So I think I would use it almost all the time! I would probably listen to music mostly when I'm on the bus, or walking somewhere, like to school. And I would use it to share music with my friends. I think I could even use it to download films and music videos. You can also use them to store your photos and other stuff. Actually, you can use it to take your own photos as well. There is no keyboard, so you just touch the screen to type and send text messages. I really want to get one because all my friends have them and I think they are so useful. But I probably have to wait until my parents buy me one. I love new technology—I'm always interested in the latest things.'

20 Look at the script and classify what the speaker said into the categories below. Then, make your own notes about the same prompt card.

	What is it?	Why is it useful? How/When would you use it?	Adjectives	Why do you want it?
Speaker				
Your notes				

21 Read the transcript again and underline all the times the speakers uses the words 'would' and 'could'.

Note that the speaker is imagining what he **would** or **could** do if he owned this possession. He doesn't actually own it but he would like to.

22 Read the following sentences. Write the letter 'I' if the sentences are 'imagining the situation' and write the letter 'T' if the sentences are 'an actual, true situation'. The first two have been done for you.

a. If I owned a sports car, I would use it to drive to university every day. I
b. I drive my sports car to university every day. T
c. My brother is famous and gives me a lot of his money.
d. My brother could give me a lot of money if he was famous.
e. I'd prefer a blackberry to a cell phone because I could write e-mails as well as send texts.
f. I use my blackberry more than my cell phone because I can write e-mails as well as send texts.

23 Using your notes from above, begin your long turn. Try to speak for the full two minutes.

Remember to speak as fluently as possible, that is, NO long pauses.

TIP
When you are talking about the functions of a technological possession, you can use the following language:

It can + verb...

It is used for + noun...

You can use it for + noun

It is useful for + noun

24 Look at the following mixed up rounding off questions for Part 2. Unscramble them to make the questions.

a. popular/friends?/many/of/they/are/with/your

____

b. often/how/use/it?/would/you

____

c. like/buy/new/do/things?/you/to Why/why not?

____

d. what/items/technological/are/other/important/you?/for
Why?

____

TIP
The rounding off questions only require a brief response, so keep your answer short and just answer the question. This is not the time for another long turn!

25 Now ask and answer the rounding off questions with your partner.

UNIT 14 Money and Finance

Focus on Part 1 of the IELTS Speaking Test

WARM-UP

1 Listen to these Part 1 sentences and repeat.

a. My parents give me an allowance to buy things I need.
b. I have a part-time job, so I make some money to spend on myself.
c. I saved money for a year, so I could buy myself a guitar.
d. I have just opened my first bank account.
e. I'm happy to lend money to my friends if they pay me back.

VOCABULARY

2 Look at the following verbs that are collocations you can use with the word 'money'. Use them to fill in the gaps in the sentences below. Use each word once. The first one has been done for you.

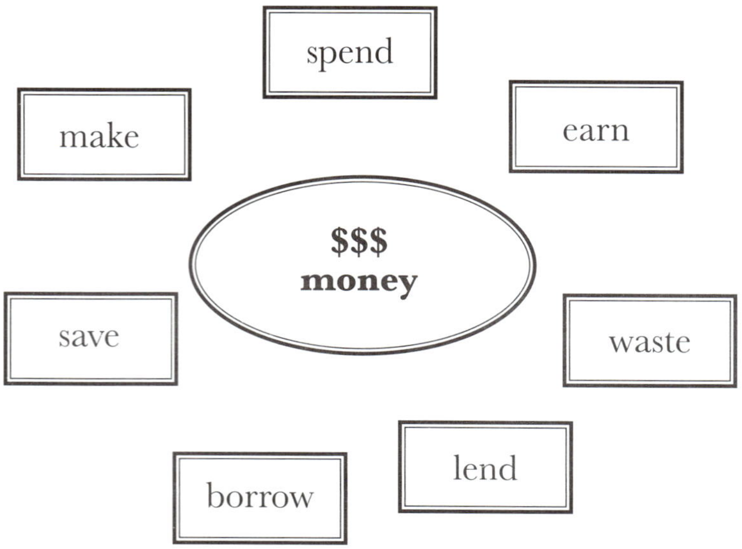

Remember:
You **borrow** money **from** someone and you **lend** money **to** someone.

a. My new job is very good. I ___earn___ twice as much money as I did in my old job.
b. I want to ________ a lot of money so that I can invest it and ________ more money.
c. Can you ________ me $100?
d. My friend ________ a lot of money. She is always buying things she doesn't really need.
e. His family ________ a lot of money from the bank to start their restaurant business.
f. I don't ________ much money on going out or shopping because I am saving for a holiday.

3 *Look at the following words and phrases in the Vocabulary Bank and check any that you don't know in your dictionary. Write the words in the table below—are they nouns, verbs or adjectives?*

Vocabulary Bank				
wallet	mean	generous	purse	pay back
loan	invest	tax	salary	bank account
wages	poor	cash	discount	pocket money
discount	bargain	allowance	price	credit card
wealthy	expensive	cheap	pricey	good value
selfish	afford	rich	ATM	cash machine

Nouns	Adjectives	Verbs
wallet	mean	pay back

4 *Listen and repeat the words.*

5 *Classify the words into 1 syllable, 2 syllable, 3 and 4 syllable words. Listen again and mark the stressed syllable in each word.*

1 syllable	2 syllables	3 syllables	4 syllables
Purse	Wallet	Allowance	

6 *Ask and answer the following Part 1 questions with your partner.*

a. When was the last time you lent someone money?
b. When did you borrow money last time?
c. Do you lend money to friends?
d. Are you good at saving money? Why/Why not?
e. Have you ever saved for something you really wanted?
f. Do you think you are a generous person?
g. Do you know any mean or selfish people?
h. Do you make good decisions with money?
i. Do you know anyone who makes bad decisions with money?
j. Have you found any bargains recently?
k. Do you receive pocket money or an allowance from your parents?
l. Do you have a job and earn your own money?
m. Do you have your own bank account?

Voiced **th** /ð/ as in 'there'
Unvoiced **th** /θ/ as in 'thank'

To make this sound, put your tongue between your teeth and release air between your top teeth and tongue. Watch your teacher.

The sound /θ/ is unvoiced. Put your hand on your throat. When you make this sound, you will not feel any vibration in this area.
To make the /ð/ sound, use voice. You will feel the vibrations in your throat.

7 *Look at the following words from the unit. Listen to the audio and divide them into /θ/ and /ð/ sounds:*

think	wealthy
thanks	something
their	although
this	MP3
that	health

/θ/ sounds	/ð/ sounds

8 *Listen and repeat the words.*

9 *Listen and repeat the following sentences paying attention to pronouncing /θ/ and /ð/ correctly.*

a. I think that he has a lot of money.
b. Although Thelma is wealthy, she is also relaxed.
c. I think that sink is dirty.
d. Thank you for that MP3 player!
e. This is that place where we thought lunch was delicious.
f. Health is more important than wealth.
g. He sank the boat before I could say thanks.

10 Circle the word you hear.

a. sink/think
b. sank/thank
c. sing/thing
d. sick/thick
e. sort/thought

11 Practise saying the pairs of words.

Focus on Part 2 of the IELTS Speaking Test

12 Listen to the speaker talking about what she spends her money on. Write down five things she buys quite often.

a. ____________ b. ____________ c. ____________
d. ____________ e. ____________

13 Look at the underlined vocabulary in the script on the last page of this unit. Read the words around each word or phrase and see if you can guess what the words mean from their context.

all sorts of things: ____________ stuff: ____________
can't live without: ____________ running out of: ____________

14 Make your own list of things you buy or have recently bought.

15 Read the following Part 2 prompt card. You have one minute to make notes on this topic.

Describe something you have bought recently.
You should say:
 what it was
 where you bought it
 whether it was good value
and explain why you bought it.

TIP
While this question looks very simple, it can be easy to run out of ideas about what to say. Remember to add extra information to make your answer longer and to make it easier to keep talking for up to two minutes.

16 Now listen to the candidate speaking and check whether he talks about something different or similar to your idea.

17 Use some of the same language to help you speak to your partner on the same topic.

- I recently bought a ______________________________.
- The __________ I bought was from a ______________________.
- I went shopping there ______________________________.
- This __________ was/was not good value, because ____________________ ______________________________.
- I really like/enjoy ______________________________, which is why I bought the ______________________________.
- I would like to buy ______________ because ______________.

Focus on Part 3 of the IELTS Speaking Test

In Part 3 of the IELTS speaking test, the examiner will ask you more abstract questions related to the Part 2 topic. This part of the test lasts for four or five minutes.

18 Read the example Part 3 questions below. Then look at each example question in more details.

a. In your country, how do people express wealth and affluence?
b. What are the advantages and disadvantages of consumerism?
c. Is society now more materialistic than it used to be in previous generations?
d. How has technology affected patterns of purchasing behaviour?

a. In your country, how do people express wealth and affluence?

This means: What do people buy to show they are rich / to show their status? For example: big houses.

Write your ideas below.

b. What are the advantages and disadvantages of consumerism?

This means: what are the advantages and disadvantages of a society that buys and sells a lot of goods, often resulting in people having more than they need?

Write your ideas below.

Advantages	Disadvantages
Good for economy	Greed

GRAMMAR

When you answer the type of question above, be sure to use contrast connectives, such as:

but / whereas / however / on the other hand

When you answer the following type of question, be aware of changes between the **past** and **present**. Choose your tenses carefully.

c. Is society now more materialistic than it used to be in previous generations?

This means: Do people think that having lots of money and possessions is the most important thing in life? Did your parents and grandparents think like this?

Write your ideas.

PAST

NOW

d. How has technology affected patterns of purchasing behaviour?

This means: Have things like the Internet changed the way we spend our money?

Write some examples below.

INTERNET → SHOPPING For example:

o ____________________

o ____________________

o ____________________

19 *Listen to the candidate answering Part 3 questions.*

Examiner: Now I'd like to move on to ask you some more general questions. Firstly, could you tell me how people express wealth and affluence in your country?

Candidate: Well, I think more and more people are choosing to show their status through the clothes they wear and the cars they drive. For example, wealthy people might wear expensive labels as a symbol of their status, or drive an expensive car to show they have lots of money. Some other people see their job as an expression of wealth, for example, a CEO or an accountant.

Examiner: And what do you see as the advantages and disadvantages of consumerism?

Candidate: I believe that consumerism is positive in terms of creating jobs and boosting the economy. I mean as people buy things, the need for production is increased, so more people are employed and so on. However, the disadvantage of consumerism is that people become too concerned about buying the latest product or item, and I think actually people can become a bit greedy. You know, they have to have what their friends have and so on.

Examiner: Okay. So thinking about that, do you believe society nowadays is more materialistic than in previous generations?

Candidate: I think so, absolutely. I mean, for my grandparents, it was totally different. They had different values, and they were probably more basic values of hard work and family. Whereas today, people might say that my generation is too spoilt, or you know, materialistic. For instance, while my grandparents might have been focused on getting enough food to feed their family, some young people today are more interested in the latest movies and fashion. It's different.

Examiner: Okay, and finally, how do you think technology has affected purchasing behaviour?

Candidate: It has changed the way people buy things, totally. Take the Internet as an example. People can buy things from all over the world, so they have much more choice. For example, I can buy a book from someone in England or a computer from a company in Hong Kong. Technology has changed shopping patterns considerably and I think it is a big improvement.

FLUENCY AND COHERENCE

20 *Ask and answer the same questions with your partner. Use your notes from the activity above and the language from the dialogue to help you.*

Q1: Now I'd like to move on to ask you some more general questions. Firstly, could you explain how people express wealth and affluence in your country?

- I think more and more people are choosing to show their status through ________.
- For example, wealthy people might ____________________ or ________ ____________________ to show that they have lots of money. Some people see ____________________ as an expression of wealth, for example ________.

Q2: And what do you see as the advantages and disadvantages of consumerism?

- I believe that consumerism is positive in terms of ________________ and ________________ ________________________.
- However, a drawback of consumerism is that ________________________________ ____.
- I think people become ________________________________.

Q3: Okay. So thinking about that, do you believe society nowadays is more materialistic than in previous generations?

- I think so/I don't think so.
- For my grandparents' generation, it was ________________________.
- Whereas today, people might say that my generation is________________________ ________________________________.
- For instance, while my grandparents might have been focused on________________ ____________ some young people today are more interested in ________________ ____________________.

Q4: Okay, and finally, how do you think technology has affected purchasing behaviour?

- It has/has not changed the way people buy things.
- Take ____________ as an example.
- ______________ so ________________ (reason/result).

Script for Activity 13:

I spend my money on all sorts of things, but I guess the main stuff would be the things I need to buy regularly, like lunch at the school cafeteria, magazines about the latest celebrity news, and music, which I can't live without. Oh, and I also buy a coffee on the way to school most days. What else… Oh yeah, I'm always running out of credit on my mobile phone, so I buy credit for that quite often.

Speaking

UNIT 15 Employment

Focus on Part 1 of the IELTS Speaking Test

WARM-UP

1 Look at these different types of jobs. Work with a partner to add some more.

2 Now think about each of the above jobs. What would you have to do every day if this was your job? The first two have been done for you as an example.

Job	Duties
nurse	look after sick people in hospital; assist doctors; record patient information; change bandages and dressings; hand out medication
mechanic	repair people's cars; check cars for safety; talk to customers
accountant	
teacher	
plumber	

3 *Listen to the following speakers talking about their job duties. Circle the job that the speaker is talking about.*

a.	dentist	doctor	nurse
b.	bus driver	postman	fireman
c.	lawyer	accountant	manager

VOCABULARY

Vocabulary Bank

Jobs: Nouns	Jobs: Verbs	Jobs: Adjectives	Qualifications	Skills & Knowledge
accountant	advise	active	apprenticeship	communication
builder	calculate	challenging	certificate	computer
bus/truck driver	check	enjoyable	course	cooking
chef	communicate	exciting	Bachelor's degree	driving
dentist	contact	full-time	diploma	flying
doctor	deliver	ideal	doctorate	foreign language
dressmaker	drive	interactive	Master's degree	listening
electrician	examine	interesting	training	maths
fireman	fix	part-time	university	medical
flight attendant	greet	safe		numerical
journalist	interact	sedentary	**Employment**	organization
lawyer	load	self-employed	employee	presentation
manager	look after	stressful	employer	reading
musician	manage	technical	employment	sales
pilot	organise	temporary	contract	speaking
police officer	prepare	varied	opportunity	teaching
postman	repair	well-paid	promotion	technical
receptionist	sort		salary	translation
scientist	teach		staff	typing
secretary			wages	writing
teacher			workforce	
tour guide			workplace	

4 Think of three different jobs you would like to do. Brainstorm each one and write words in the correct columns below. Use the Vocabulary Bank and your dictionary to help you.

What is the job?	What would you have to do every day?	What skills or qualifications would you need?	Why would you like to do this job?
e.g. secretary	e.g. type letters, answer the phone, make appointments, make travel bookings, send and collect mail	e.g. typing, computer, reading, listening, speaking, foreign language	e.g. interesting, varied, meet different people
1.			
2.			
3.			

5 Now compare your lists of words with a partner. Do you have any of the same words? Did you choose any of the same jobs?

PRONUNCIATION

6 Listen to these job titles. They are all ***compound nouns*** *or* ***noun + noun****. In each case, underline the word or syllable that carries the main stress. The first one has been done for you.*

●
bank teller
bus driver
checkout operator
dressmaker
fireman
flight attendant
police officer
postman
tour guide
travel agent

In compound nouns, the main stress is usually on the first syllable. In two-word phrases made up of **noun + noun**, the main stress is usually on the first word.

7 Now listen and repeat the job titles.

GRAMMAR

Like or **would like**

8 Listen to two speakers and circle the correct answer to each question.

What is Speaker 1 talking about? — things she enjoys doing now **or** something she wants to do in the future

What is Speaker 2 talking about? — things he enjoys doing now **or** something he wants to do in the future

9 Listen again and complete the sentences.

a. I really __________ __________ with people. I __________ __________ __________ them find solutions to their problems.

b. I__________ really __________ __________ __________ a TV news reporter.

> To talk about things we enjoy doing **now**, we use:
>
> I like doing *or* I like to do
>
> To talk about something we want to do in the **future**, we use:
>
> I would do (I'd do) *or* I would like to do (I'd like to do)

10 Complete the following sentences using your own ideas. Then work with a partner and take turns to ask and answer the questions below.

In my spare time, I like...
In the future, I'd like...

Questions:
What do you like doing in your spare time?
What would you like to do in the future?

11 Read the prompt card. Listen to a candidate talking on this topic. As you listen, circle the correct answer below, a, b, or c.

Describe your ideal job.
You should say:
what the job is
what you would have to do every day
what skills or qualifications you would need
and explain why you would like this job.

i. What would the speaker's ideal job be?
   a. airline pilot
   b. flight attendant
   c. travel agent

ii. Which of the following duties would she have to do?
   a. organize flights and accommodation
   b. welcome passengers on board
   c. check in passengers

iii. Which one of the following skills would she need?
   a. communication
   b. maths
   c. technical

iv. What is one reason why would this be her ideal job?
   a. She likes doing the same thing every day.
   b. She likes doing lots of different things.
   c. She likes learning maths and physics.

Put it all together

12 Look back at the prompt card and make notes using your own ideas.

What the job is:

____

____

* What you would have to do every day:

____

____

* What skills or qualifications you would need:

____

____

* I would like this job because:

____

____

13 Work with a partner. Take turns speaking for 1 to 2 minutes on the topic. As you are listening to your partner's talk, think of one or two suitable questions that you could ask at the end.

Focus on Part 3 of the IELTS Speaking Test

14 Look at these statements about what the employment situation will be like in the future. Check the meanings of any new words.

In 50 years from now, everyone will be expected to have a university degree.

In years to come, we won't have to leave home to work. We'll just switch on our home computer.

Over the next 20 years, women will achieve equal pay with men.

Over the course of this century, thousands of new jobs that don't even exist today will be created.

15 With a partner, discuss whether or not you agree with the above statements.

FLUENCY AND COHERENCE

In Part 3 of the Speaking Test, you will often be asked to talk about future trends and changes.

16 Look at the following phrases for referring to the future.

In the future...

In the next five years...

Over the course of this century...

Over the next decade...

In years to come...

In 50 years from now...

Now listen to five different speakers' statements and match their statements to the future time phrases below. The first one has been done for you.

A. Over the next decade
B. In the future
C. In 50 years from now
D. In years to come
E. In the next millennium

i. ____B____ many people will become self-employed.
ii. __________ we'll only have to work four-day weeks.
iii. __________ we won't have to leave home to work.
iv. __________ there will be hundreds of new jobs created in IT.
v. __________ humans will be replaced by machines in many jobs.

Note: To make predictions about the future, we use *will* or *won't* + *the base form* of the verb.

17 *Work with a partner. Take turns to make the following predictions about employment in the future. Use* ***will*** *or* ***won't*** *according to your own opinion.*

Women / achieve equal pay with men.

e.g. Women will achieve equal pay with men.

a. The majority of people / have two jobs.

b. Everyone / have to work more hours in the day.

c. Salaries / increase significantly.

d. Most people / sit in front of a computer screen all day.

e. Machines / replace humans in many jobs.

f. People / have to leave their houses to work.

18 Now look at the future time phrases in the box below. When do you think the above things will happen? With a partner, take turns to make the above predictions using the time phrases in the box.

Over the next decade	In the future	In 50 years from now
In years to come	In the next millennium	Over the course of this century
In 2050	In 20 years' time	Hundreds of years from now

19 Look at the following questions. Note down all of the vocabulary items you will need to make predictions about employment in the future. Use the Vocabulary Bank at the beginning of this unit and some of the useful phrases and collocations in the box below as well as your dictionary to help you if necessary.

a. What do you think the average workplace will be like in the future?
b. What do you think the situation of women employees will be like in the future?
c. How do you think that jobs will be different in the future?
d. What will be the role of machines in the workplace of the future?
e. Do you think that the length of the working week will change in the future?
f. Do you think that salaries will increase enough to cover the cost of living?
g. Do you think that people will need more training and qualifications?

Useful Phrases & Collocations		
annual leave	on-the-job training	to argue a case
career advancement	pay parity	to give someone advice on/about something
employment agency	shift work	to give someone the opportunity to do something
employment contract	sick leave	to let someone know something
employment relations	situations vacant	to solve a problem
hours of work	social club	
job pressure	temp / temping agency	
job security	work conditions	
job title	work experience	

20 Now work with a partner. Take turns to ask and answer the questions above. Make sure that you give your own opinion and extend your answer to include examples or reasons.

Speaking

UNIT 16 Commodities

Focus on Part 2 of the IELTS Speaking Test

WARM-UP

Commodities are anything that can be sold or traded. This unit focuses on commodities such as agricultural products (crops, meat) and natural resources (gold, fuel, energy, etc.).

1 *Look at these different types of jobs. Work with a partner to add some more.*

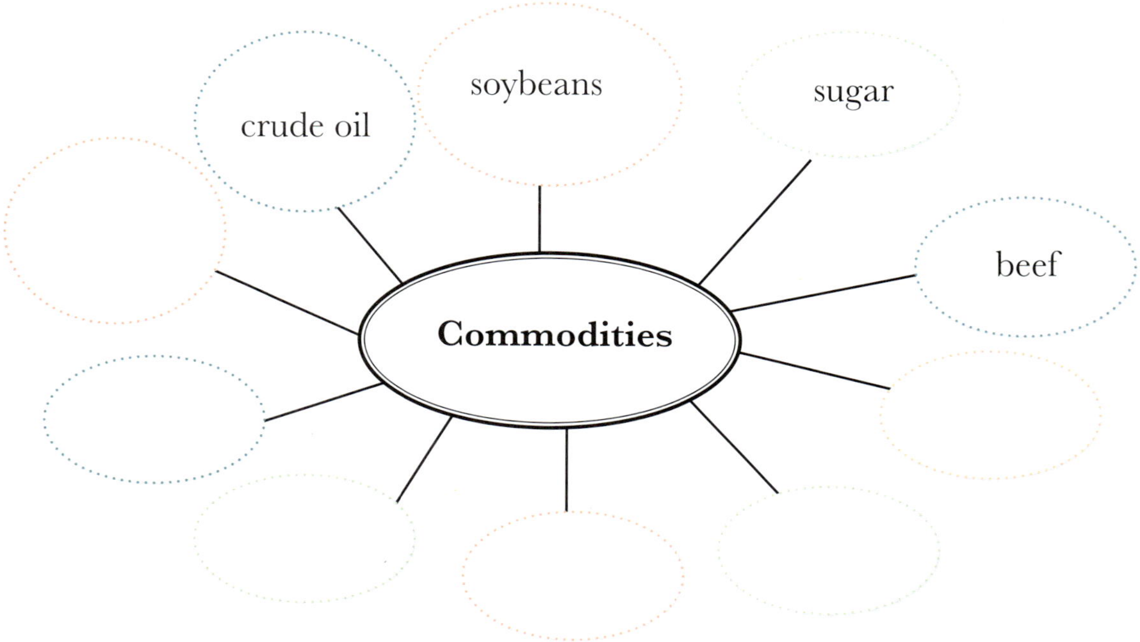

2 *Listen to the following speakers talking about different commodities. Circle the commodity they are speaking about.*

a.	gold	beef	wool
b.	wheat	coffee beans	barley
c.	cotton	copper	petrol

VOCABULARY

Vocabulary Bank				
Commodities				
Nouns	Verbs	Adjectives	Markets	Phrases & Collocations
agriculture	cultivate	agricultural	decrease	*Noun phrases*
barley	develop	important	demand	barley crops
beef	export	main	distribution	copper mine
coal	extract	necessary	drop	coal mine
cocoa	grow	primary	fluctuations	energy reserves
coffee beans	harvest	processed	increase	environmental
copper	import	unprocessed	price	considerations
corn	manufacture	useful	production	intensive farming
cotton	mine	vital	shortage	natural resources
crop	plant		staples (food)	petrol refinery
crude oil	process		subsidy	price drop
energy	produce		supply	price increase
fuel	refine			raw products
gas	sow			supply and
gold	weave			demand
harvest				
metal				*Verb phrases*
natural gas				build mines
palm oil				cultivate corn /
petroleum				wheat
platinum				mine (v) copper /
rice				gold / silver / coal
rubber				plant corn/seeds/
silver				crops
soybeans				refine oil
wheat				spin wool
wool				weave textiles

3 *Think of three different natural resource commodities that are important to your country or to you in your everyday life. Brainstorm each one and write words in the correct columns below. Use the Vocabulary Bank and your dictionary to help you.*

What is the commodity?	Which country / countries does it come from?	Where can you buy it?	Why is this commodity important to you / your country?
e.g. oil	e.g. Iran, Iraq, Saudi Arabia, Algeria, Venezuela	e.g. service stations	e.g. main fuel for vehicles
1.			
2.			
3.			

4 *Now compare your lists of words with a partner. Do you have any of the same words? Did you choose any of the same commodities?*

PRONUNCIATION

Linking

This is so important in English! There are three ways that native speakers link words:

(i) Consonant + vowel *or* vowel + consonant

5 *Listen and repeat. Focus on linking the final sound[1] of the first word to the first sound of the second word.*

cru**de o**il
depen**d o**n
diese**l e**ngine
ge**t a**round
iro**n o**re
pal**m o**il
pri**ce i**ncrease
barl**ey c**rop
copp**er m**ine
energ**y s**ource
gr**ow c**rops
rubb**er t**ree
sug**ar c**ane
s**ow s**eeds

6 *Listen and repeat the sentences. Focus on linking the underlined sounds.*

Cru**de oi**l **is an i**mportan**t e**nerg**y s**ource.
Many people depen**d o**n th**eir c**ars **to g**e**t a**round.
O**ur m**ain crop**s are r**ubb**er t**ree**s a**nd sug**ar c**ane.

---

[1] Note: Many words end in a written vowel (usually "e"), but the final sound is a consonant (e.g. increase, mine, trade). Likewise, many words end in a written consonant (often the letter "r"), but the final **sound** (in many varieties of English) is a vowel (e.g. copper, rubber, sugar).

(ii) Consonant + consonant

This type of linking often occurs when one word ends in the consonant sound /t/, /d/ or /n/, and the following word begins with /m/, /b/ or /p/.

7 *Listen and repeat. Focus on hearing and pronouncing the final consonant sound of each word.*

cotton	export	gold
plant	refined	iron

8 *Now listen to the following phrases. Notice how the final consonant of the first word is changed to become similar to the first consonant sound of the second word. In addition, sometimes the final consonant sound may be dropped, as in the case of small 'grammar words' like 'and'.*

cotto**n p**roducts	gol**d m**ine	iro**n b**ar
expor**t m**arket	plan**t b**arley	refine**d p**etroleum
wheat an**d b**arley		

9 *Listen again and repeat the above phrases.*

(iii) Vowel + vowel

When one word ends in a vowel sound and the next one begins with a vowel sound, native speakers often insert a /j/, /w/ or /r/ sound between these two vowels.

10 *Listen. The following pairs of words are joined by a /j/ sound.*

bu**y a**pples	coff**ee or** cocoa
suppl**y a**nd demand	rel**y o**n

11 *Now listen and repeat the above phrases.*

12 *Listen. The following pairs of words are joined by a /w/ sound.*

gr**ow a**pples	n**ew a**nd used
s**ow a** field	t**oo i**nefficient

13 *Now listen and repeat the above phrases.*

14 *Listen. The following pairs of words are joined by a /r/ sound.*

ca**r e**xports	coppe**r a**lloy
sha**re i**ssue	suga**r a**nd salt

15 *Now listen and repeat the above phrases.*

16 Work with a partner. Decide if the following words are linked by a /j/, /w/ or /r/ sound. Circle the correct answer.

a.	kno**w a** market	/j/	/w/	/r/
b.	fou**r a**pples	/j/	/w/	/r/
c.	yo**u a**nd I	/j/	/w/	/r/
d.	w**e e**xport rice	/j/	/w/	/r/
e.	compa**re i**tems	/j/	/w/	/r/
f.	the**y i**mport coffee	/j/	/w/	/r/

17 Listen and check your answers.

18 Now listen and repeat the above phrases.

GRAMMAR

Relative Clauses

19 Work with a partner. Complete the sentences using the correct relative clauses from the box.

which export coffee beans	which is used to make bread
which comes from sugar cane	that's important to me in my everyday life

a. A commodity ______________________________ is rice.
b. Many countries ______________________ are situated in Africa and South America.
c. Sugar, ______________________________, exists in many different forms.
d. Wheat, ________________________, is grown in a variety of climates and soil types.

20 Now listen and check your answers.

A **relative clause** usually starts with **who**, **that or which** and comes immediately after the noun it is describing.

21 Work with a partner. Practise joining the pairs of sentences below to make single sentences with a main clause and a relative clause.

For example:

The wool is exported. The wool comes from sheep. →
The wool that comes from sheep is exported.

a. Petrol is becoming more and more expensive. Petrol is used to fuel the majority of motor vehicles.
b. Gold is extracted from goldmines or riverbeds. Gold is a precious metal.
c. Coffee beans are roasted to bring out the flavour. The coffee beans are imported from Africa.
d. Copper is mined in the United States and Chile. Copper has been used by man for 10,000 years.
e. The rice is of the long-grained variety. We use the rice to make this special dish.

Put it all together

Look at the prompt card below.

Describe a commodity that is important in your everyday life.
You should say:
what it is
which country it comes from
where you can buy it
and explain why this commodity is important to you.

22 *Listen to a candidate talking on this topic. As you listen, answer the questions and circle the correct answer, A or B.*

i. Which commodity is he talking about?
A. Platinum B. Petroleum
ii. Does he know where his country imports the raw product from?
A. He's sure B. He's not sure
iii. Where does he buy the refined product from?
A. Service station B. Supermarket
iv. Why is this commodity important to him?
A. For his work B. For his hobby

23 *Look at the prompt card and prepare for your long turn by making notes using your own ideas. Work with a partner as you each do your long turn.*

Focus on Part 3 of the IELTS Speaking Test

24 *Look at these statements about how we can solve some of the problems relating to the production and distribution of commodities. Check the meanings of any new words.*

We need to find alternative vehicle fuels that can be cheaply produced.

It's important that we start looking in other places to locate more of these natural energy reserves.

It's a matter of getting around the wars, politics and corruption that prevent the distribution of staples to the general population.

In the future, I think it'll be necessary for us to rely on science to help us produce faster-growing crops if we want to have enough.

We have to provide food subsidies to people who can't afford it.

25 *With a partner, discuss what problems these people are talking about.*

FLUENCY AND COHERENCE

In Part 3 of the speaking test, you will often be asked to talk about problems and solutions.

26 *Look at the following phrases for suggesting solutions*

We need to...

We have to...

In the future, we'll need to...

It's a matter of...

It's important that we...

We should...

27 *Now listen to five different answers to the questions below. Match each answer with an appropriate question. Write the letter A – E of the correct question next to the numbers i – v. The first one has been done for you.*

A. How can we solve the problem of increasing petrol prices?
B. How can we solve the problem of declining energy reserves?
C. How can we solve the problem of food distribution in some parts of the world?
D. How can we solve the problem of increasing food prices?
E. Do you think that we will be able to produce enough staples, such as rice, to feed the world's population in the future?

i. D　　ii. ______　　iii. ______

iv. ______　　v. ______

28 *Work with a partner. Take turns to suggest the solutions to the problems.*

For example:

How can we solve the problem of food distribution in some parts of the world?

matter / get around the wars, politics and corruption that prevent the distribution of staples to the general population

It's a matter of getting around the wars, politics and corruption that prevent the distribution of staples to the general population.

a. How can we solve the problem of increasing petrol prices?

need / find alternative vehicle fuels that can be cheaply produced

b. How can we solve the problem of declining energy reserves?

important / start looking in other places to locate more of these natural energy reserves

c. How can we solve the problem of increasing food prices?

have / provide food subsidies to people who can't afford it

d. Do you think that we will be able to produce enough staples, such as rice, to feed the world's population in the future?

In / future / think / necessary / rely on science to help us produce faster-growing crops if we want to have enough.

29 *Look at the following questions. Note down all of the vocabulary items you will need to give* ***your own*** *solutions to the problems. Use the Vocabulary Bank and your dictionary to help you if necessary.*

a. How can we solve the problem of increasing petrol prices?
b. How can we solve the problem of declining energy reserves?
c. How can we solve the problem of food distribution in some parts of the world?
d. How can we solve the problem of increasing food prices?
e. Do you think that we will be able to produce enough staples, such as rice, to feed the world's population in the future?

30 *Now work with a partner. Take turns to ask and answer the questions above. Make sure that you give your own opinion.*

UNIT 17 Population

Focus on Part 2 of the IELTS Speaking Test

WARM-UP

1 *Place each of the following adjectives in the correct place on the concept map below. An example has been done for you.*

slim	cruel	kind	overweight	athletic
lazy	cold-hearted	energetic	mean	lively
gentle	tolerant	practical	charming	aggressive
relaxed	muscular	anxious	enthusiastic	ugly
humble	bald	warm	good-looking	

VOCABULARY

2 *Mark each of the adjectives in the 'Personality/Appearance' column of the Vocabulary Bank on the next page with an A for Appearance or a P for Personality.*

Vocabulary Bank

Personality/Appearance	General	Collocations
Adjectives	life expectancy	to have a good/great sense of humour
slim	longevity	
cruel	lifespan	
athletic	diet	to have a low/high standard of living
lazy	quality of life	
warm	standard of living	
cold-hearted	alcoholism	rural areas
overweight	poverty	urban areas
energetic	resource	
kind	population	to be well off
lively	government	to be better off
gentle	civil war	
bald	education	to be badly off
enthusiastic	health care	to be worse off
deceitful	disease	
anxious	epidemic	
mean	wages	
relaxed	citizens	
muscular		
aggressive		
charming	*Adjectives*	
humble	developed	
optimistic	industrialised	
intolerant	rural	
honest	urban	
generous	wealthy	
patient	worst-affected	
	nutritious	
Nouns—appearance		
wrinkles		
freckles		
dimples		
pimples		

When learning vocabulary, it can be helpful to group words together.

Words for describing character or personality can be grouped into

- good qualities
- bad qualities

Words for describing appearance can be grouped together as

- positive
- negative

Words with similar meaning can be grouped together

For example:

lively, energetic

Words with opposite meaning can be grouped together

For example:

kind—cruel

3 *Look at the left column of the Vocabulary Bank and try putting words into the following groups or categories. Some have been done for you. Add any other words you know to the Personality and Appearance groups.*

Personality	Appearance	Find words with Similar meanings	Find words with Opposite meanings
Good Qualities: *Lively*	Positive: *Slim*	*Mean –* *Energetic –* *Gentle –* *Athletic –*	*Overweight –* *Kind –* *Warm –* *Deceitful –* *Relaxed –* *Patient –*
Bad Qualities: *Lazy*	Negative: *Ugly*		

4 *Study the following questions:*

- What's he like?
- What does he look like?

Which question wants you to talk about the man's appearance?

For example:

'Well, he's short, fat and bald...'

Which question wants you to talk about his personality or character?

For example:

'Well, he's very serious and sometimes he's quite mean...'

5 *Think of someone you know well. Tell your partner whether the person you're thinking of is male or female. Then, take turns asking:*

- What's he/she like?
- What does he/she look like?

Use words from the **Vocabulary Bank** to help you answer.
(Generally your answers to the first question will be **P** for 'Personality' words, and your answers to the second question will be **A** for 'Appearance' words.)

6 *Look at the topic card below and think about how you would structure your talk in Part 2 of the Speaking Test.*

- Use the prompts to help you organise your ideas.
- Just following the prompts will give your talk a good structure.
- You will be marked on the organisation of your ideas in the exam.

Describe an old person you admire.
You should say:
  who he/she is
  what he/she looks like
  what his/her best qualities are
and explain why you admire this person.

Put it all together

7 *Listen to a candidate talking on this topic. As you listen, match each section of the talk with its content.*

Introducing your choice	Section _____
Describing physical appearance	Section _____
Describing character or personality	Section _____
Explaining the reason for your choice	Section _____

8 *Look back at the prompt card and make notes about an old person you admire. Using your notes, talk to your partner for one to two minutes about the old person you admire.*

Focus on Part 3 of the IELTS Speaking Test

In Part 3 you will often be expected to **make suggestions**. You may not be sure of your ideas, so you will need to learn how to express uncertainty and possibility.

9 *Look at the chart below. You can see that life expectancy[1] in New Zealand is 80 years. Try to predict the life expectancy for the other countries in the table. Then check your partner's chart. Do you agree?*

Country	Years	Country	Years
Botswana[2]		China	
Russia		New Zealand	80
Peru		Japan	

10 *Now, work with your partner to discuss these questions:*

- What do you know about these countries?
- What factors do you think influence life expectancy?

11 *Listen to the audio recording and check the information you have written in the chart. Does any of the information surprise you? Why? / Why not?*

PRONUNCIATION

English speakers do not give equal stress to all the words in a sentence. Only the content words are stressed. These are the words that give **new** or **important** information in a sentence. They are usually nouns, verbs and adjectives. Most of the other words are unstressed because they give less important information or they simply provide the grammar structure which joins all the information together.

12 *Listen to the end of the life expectancy audio recording again and underline the words in each sentence that carry the main stress. Two have been done for you.*

'Terrible isn't it? I know that about two thirds of Botswana is desert, but I also know it has a great natural resource, diamonds, so it's a relatively wealthy country and it only has a small population. I've also heard that it has a good system of government and there is no civil war or fighting. It even has free education and health care for all its citizens.'
'Why do they die so young then?' 'Disease. The AIDS epidemic. It's the worst-affected country in the world!'

13 *Read the sentences above and stress the underlined words.*

14 *Practise saying the following sentences stressing the words in bold. Remember the stressed words will be spoken slightly louder and longer than the others.*

- There's a **lot** of **poverty** in **Peru**.
- It's a very **poor** country.

1 The length of time a person is normally likely to live.

2 A country in the Kalahari Desert region of southern Africa.

- They have quite a **low standard** of **living**.
- What about New **Zealand**?
- They've got plenty of **clean**, **fresh air**.
- I've also heard that it has a **good system** of **government**.
- The government takes a lot of **taxes** though.
- What are the **people** like?
- On the whole, they are quite well-**educated**.
- I've heard they're very **friendly**, **too**.

GRAMMAR

Modal verbs: would, could, may or **might** to express **uncertainty, possibility** and to make **suggestions**.

15 *Look at the script of the audio recording about the life expectancy chart. Underline the modal verbs.*

'Hey, have you seen this chart? Guess which country has the highest life expectancy in the world?'

'I know the answer to that question: it's Japan. 82 years is how long the average Japanese can expect to live. ...Why is that, do you think?'

'I don't know for sure but their diet might have a lot to do with it. They eat lots of fish and vegetables.'

'Oh. Do New Zealanders have a good diet too?'

'As far as I know, they eat too much meat and cheese so it's not exactly a healthy diet ... lots of protein but probably too much fat. Their quality of life would be good though. New Zealand's part of the developed world, but it's not really an industrialised country, so they've got plenty of clean, fresh air.'

'That could be the reason for their longevity, I suppose ... I thought it might be because they play a lot of sport and get lots of exercise. Look, I see life expectancy in China is pretty high.'

'Yes. ***72****. I think that's the highest it's ever been... higher now than Peru where people only live to be 70 on average. I have heard that there is a lot of poverty in Peru, in both urban and rural areas. Many of the workers are paid very low wages so they may not be able to afford nutritious food or proper health care... and Russians are even worse off; they can only expect to live to* ***65****!'*

'Too much vodka!'

'I don't know about that... but alcoholism could be a factor. Seriously, I think they have quite a low standard of living, you know, things like the quality of housing and the amount of food available. Even so, their life expectancy is nearly double that of Botswana.'

'I don't think I've heard of Botswana before. Where's that?'

'Africa. People in Botswana only live on average to the age of ***34****!'*

'That's awful!'

'Terrible isn't? I know that about two thirds of Botswana is desert, but I also know it has a great natural resource, diamonds, so it's a relatively wealthy country and it only has a small population, less than ***2*** *million. I've also heard that it has a good system of government and there is no civil war or fighting. It even has free education and health care for all its citizens.'*

'Why do they die so young then?'

'Disease. The AIDS epidemic. It's the worst-affected country in the world!'

Modal verbs: When making **suggestions**, we use **may** or **might** to talk about **possibility. Might** is more common. We also use **could** to talk about what is **possible**.

For example:

Their diet **might** have a lot to do with it.	= perhaps it does, perhaps it doesn't
You **could** be right.	= perhaps you are, perhaps you aren't

In the **negative**, we use **may not** and **might not** or **mightn't**.

For example:

They **may not** be able to afford nutritious food.
They **may not** have had a good education.
They **might not** eat a healthy diet.
They **mightn't** have had good health care when they were young.

However, **couldn't** is different from **may not** and **might not**.

For example:

They **mightn't** have had good health care.	= perhaps they did, perhaps they didn't (in other words, I'm not sure)
They **couldn't** have had good health care.	= it's **not possible**

When we **imagine** a situation, we use **would**.

For example:

Their quality of life **would** be good. = I imagine it is.

16 *With a partner, use the prompts to help you say sentences with **may, might, could, would** to express your uncertainty or what you imagine.*

For example:

Perhaps they are poor.

a. Perhaps they are wealthy.
b. Perhaps they are sick.
c. Perhaps alcoholism is a factor.
d. I imagine it was a good place to live.
e. Perhaps the climate is a factor.
f. Perhaps the water is not safe to drink.
g. I imagine there is a lot of fighting.
h. I imagine they were better off.
i. Perhaps there was a lot of disease.
j. Perhaps they don't have warm houses.

The same modal verbs (**would, might** and **could**) are also used for talking about something that may or may not happen in the **future**.
If we are making **predictions**, we use **would**.

For example:

A: How **would** countries cope with more and more old people?
B: I think these countries **would** need more hospitals and aged care facilities. (= old people's homes)

If we are less certain, we can **speculate** using **might** or **could**.

For example:

A: If world population continues to increase, will humans move to other planets?
B: I think they **might** do this but not in the near future. I think it **could** be possible next century.

FLUENCY AND COHERENCE

17 *Look at the examiner's questions below. Have you got enough ideas and vocabulary to answer them? In the exam, you will not be given time to prepare your answers to Part 3 questions. However, it is important to spend extra time in the classroom brainstorming ideas. Add to the ideas in the answer bubbles.*

Examiner: *'Well, you've been telling me about an old person you admire... Now, let's talk about the aging population of the world ...'*

'Why do you think life expectancy is increasing in many countries?'	better diet... less physical labour... better medical technology... medicine...
'If human lifespans continue to lengthen, in what ways will our society change?'	slower pace of life ....
'Let's move on to talk about population growth ... 'Not only is the world's population increasing, but much of the population is moving from the countryside to the city. What kinds of problems will very large cities face in the future?'	infrastructure... employment... ....

18 *With a partner, ask and answer the questions above. Give full answers. Use the modal verbs to express possibility and uncertainty and remember to stress the most important word(s) in the sentence.*

Speaking

UNIT 18 International Events

Focus on Part 2 of the IELTS Speaking Test

WARM-UP

1 *With a partner make a list of all the Olympic sports you can think of.*

---------------------	---------------------	---------------------
---------------------	---------------------	---------------------
---------------------	---------------------	---------------------

2 *With a different partner, compare lists. How many more sports can you add to your list?*

3 *Working with a partner again, put the sports on your lists into these 3 categories:*

Individual sports (sports you can play or do on your own)	Sports you can play or do against one other person	Team sports (sports you do or play in a team)

4 *Are there any sports that you would like to do or play? Tell your partner which ones and why you would like to do or play them.*

5 *Which sports do you prefer to watch? Why?*

VOCABULARY

Vocabulary Bank

Sports	Other Nouns & Verbs	Collocations
athletics	to postpone / to delay	individual sports
badminton	to impress	team sports
basketball	to update	traffic congestion
boxing	to upgrade	to make a profit
cycling	to affect	to make a loss
diving	to outweigh	remote video monitoring
football	to volunteer	public facilities
golf	volunteer (n)	public transportation system
gymnastics	to inconvenience	in the short term
hockey	inconvenience (n)	in the long term
horse-racing	foreigner	to develop closer (...) ties with
ice-skating	opponent	to develop closer relations with
motor-racing	status	cultural ties / relations
riding	infrastructure	economic ties / relations
rugby	influx	business ties / relations
skiing	inhabitants	international relations
snooker	disruption	
squash	conference	
surfing	stadium	
swimming	spectators	
tennis	media	
volleyball	restriction	
weightlifting	hygiene	
windsurfing	athlete	
	obstacle	
	accommodation	
	construction	
	expenditure	
	corruption	
	competition	

6 Look at the cue card and make notes alongside each prompt in the chart below.

Describe a major sporting event that has taken place in your country.
You should say:
  what it was
  when and where it took place
  what happened
and explain why the event was (or is) important.

Event ....
When? ....
Where? ....
What happened? ....
Important because ....
....

7 Give your talk to your partner. As you listen to your partner talking, take notice of any hesitations or long pauses.

8 Why did you (or your partner) hesitate? Was it:

- to think of ideas?
- to think about grammatical accuracy?
- to recall vocabulary?

Speaking fluently means to speak smoothly and to be able to continue with just a few natural pauses. If you stop frequently, constantly repeat yourself, have long periods of silence or stop completely before the time is up, this will lower your score.
Speaking fluently does not mean speaking quickly. Speaking too fast will lower your score too. The aim is to speak at a natural speed, neither too fast nor too slow.

In Part 2 of the Test, the topics are usually familiar and you have had time to prepare some information so you should not be stopping to think of ideas. It is more likely that you have paused to concentrate on grammatical accuracy or to recall vocabulary. Practising the grammar points in this speaking book will help you with accuracy.

If you cannot remember the English **vocabulary** you need, do not pause for too long. Instead, avoid the difficult word and use words which you do know, even if they are much simpler. Using other words, with a similar meaning, is called **paraphrasing**. This skill is recognised in the test and you will get credit for it.

For example:

They <u>postponed</u> the rowing race because it was too windy.
They <u>delayed</u>... /<u>put off</u> ... /<u>changed the time of</u> the rowing race because it was too windy.

9 *Think of ways you can **paraphrase** the underlined expressions in the following sentences. Sometimes you will have to change other parts of the sentence, too.*

a. The Olympic Games' organising committee used many volunteers to help foreigners find their way around the city.
b. There are many arguments against hosting a large event in our city.
c. Countries which host international events should have an infrastructure that can cope with the expected influx of visitors.
d. Large events often mean a lot of traffic congestion in and around the city.
e. The local inhabitants are often inconvenienced by the disruption.
f. However, the benefits far outweigh the disadvantages.

10 *Take turns with a partner. Student A reads sentences a–f and Student B repeats each sentence avoiding the underlined words and using paraphrases instead.*

Student B starts his/her sentence by saying: **'You mean...'**

For example:

'**You mean** the Olympic Games' organising committee used **unpaid workers** to help **visitors from abroad** find their way around the city.'

11 *Give your talk on a **major sporting event** again. This time, focus on fluency. Speak at a reasonable pace and try to keep going. If you get stuck for words, paraphrase.*

PRONUNCIATION

Focus stress: Normally the content, or information, words in a sentence are stressed. However, speakers of English can choose a stronger stress to highlight any word in a sentence. This stronger stress is called **focus stress** and is used to put special attention on one important part of the message. It is the main stress in a message.

The stress system in English

Focus stress	=	Main stress
Information words	=	Strong stress
Other words	=	Weak stress

Focus stress can be on **any** word. It will be louder and longer than the other stresses.
Look at this sentence: **We flew to Beijing for the Olympic Games**.

12 *Say the sentence with normal sentence stress (strong stress on information words). Listen to the model, mark the stress, and say it again.*

13 Now listen to these six examples of the same sentence said with different focus stress. Discuss with your partner what the speaker wants the listener to focus on in each sentence.

a. **We** flew to Beijing for the Olympic Games.
b. We **flew** to Beijing for the Olympic Games.
c. We flew **to** Beijing for the Olympic Games.
d. We flew to **Beijing** for the Olympic Games.
e. We flew to Beijing for the **Olympic** Games.
f. We flew to Beijing for the Olympic **Games**.

14 Repeat the sentences with the correct focus stress.

In the IELTS Speaking Test, you can use focus stress for emphasis and to make your meaning clear. You can also **listen** for focus stress to help you understand what it is in particular that the examiner wants you to focus on.

Put it all together

15 Here is the prompt card again but the word 'sporting' has been deleted. You now have a different topic—a major event in your country—even though the prompts are the same.

> Describe a major event that has taken place in your country.
> You should say:
> what it was
> when and where it took place
> what happened
> and explain why the event was (or is) important.

Note: an 'event' can be a planned and organised occasion, for example, a big international conference, or it can be something unusual or important that has happened, such as a flood or an earthquake.

Take some time to make notes on your new topic and then speak to your partner for one to two minutes concentrating on fluency and paraphrasing if necessary.

Event ....
When? ....
Where? ....
What happened? ....
Important because ....
....
....

Focus on Part 3 of the IELTS Speaking Test

In Part 3, the topic of **events** might be expanded and developed into a discussion of more general aspects of **international events**.

GRAMMAR

In Part 3 answers you will often be expected to give reasons, to say **why** something is done, what is the **purpose**. There are several ways to express purpose.

Infinitive of purpose: **Verb + to + infinitive**[1]

They do it
... ***to impress*** *other countries.*
... ***to raise*** *their status.*
... ***to attract*** *overseas visitors.*

OR: **+ for + noun**

They do it
...***for*** *national pride.*
...***for*** *economic reasons.*
...***for*** *profit.*
...***for*** the status.

OR: **so (that) + modal (can/could/, will/would)**

They do it
... ***so that*** *they* ***can*** *impress other countries.*
... ***so that*** *they* ***can*** *attract visitors.*
... ***so that*** *they* ***will*** *make a lot of money.*

They did it
... ***so that*** *they* ***could*** *make a profit.*
... ***so that*** *they* ***would*** *improve international relations.*

When the purpose is negative, use ***so (that)*** + ***won't/wouldn't.***

For example:

The officials issued maps ***so that*** *athletes and visitors* ***wouldn't*** *get lost.*
He's removing the obstacle, ***so*** *she* ***won't*** *fall over.*

16 Practise using the language above. Use the words in brackets to answer the questions. The first one has been done for you.

a. Why did they build such a big stadium? (large number of spectators)
—They built a big stadium so that it can hold a large number of spectators.
b. Why did they hold a press conference? (update the media)

---

1 In writing, or more formal contexts, you can use 'in order to' + infinitive.

c. Why was there traffic restriction? (reduce air pollution)
d. Why did they use remote video monitoring? (check food hygiene)
e. Why did they build special ramps? (wheelchairs)

17 Listen to the script and identify the various ways the candidate gives reasons in answer to the examiner's two questions.

'Can you suggest reasons why governments host international events?'

'I think there are a number of reasons for this. As far as I can see, the main purpose is to impress other countries, ... to raise their status in the world ... and maybe to improve international relations... I also believe governments like to host big events so that they can attract overseas visitors who will spend a lot of money... Yes, they do it for profit, as well, I think.'

'Any country which decides to hold a large international event will need to spend more money on infrastructure. Why?'

'Spending on infrastructure will be necessary to upgrade public facilities. They will need to build more hotels, of course, for accommodation. They will also need a good public transportation system so that visitors can get around the city easily.'

FLUENCY AND COHERENCE

18 Practise the language you have learned by answering the examiner's questions, giving reasons to support your answers. There are some ideas to help you in the bubbles but you can use your own ideas.

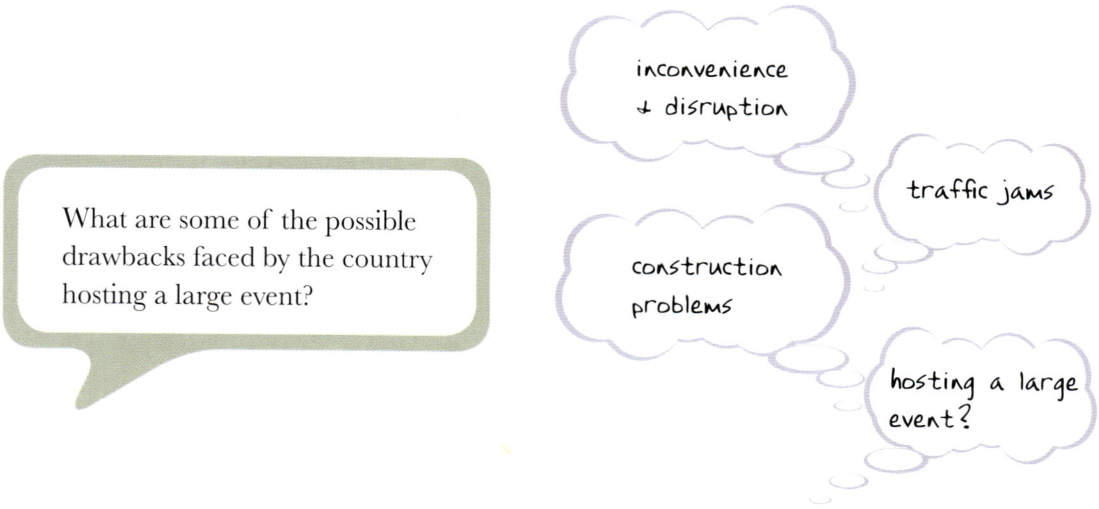

What are the main problems — affecting international sport today, in your opinion?

drugs

cost

Do you think international sport competitions are more likely to divide countries or bring them closer together?

Well, in the short term, competitions are likely to divide countries, because there will be winners and losers so ...

... but, in the long term, they might develop closer cultural ties or closer business and economic relations because ...

19 Now, with books closed, listen to the audio recording of the examiner's questions. After each question, take turns with your partner to try to give a full answer without too much hesitation. If you cannot remember the vocabulary you want, paraphrase. Make a note each time your partner pauses for more than 2 seconds or uses too much repetition and give your partner feedback.

Speaking

UNIT 19 Communication

Focus on Part 1 of the IELTS Speaking Test

WARM-UP

1 With a partner, ask and answer these questions:

- How long have you had your mobile phone?
- How often do you use it?
- What do you mostly use it for? (text messaging, talking, taking photos...)
- Which do you use more often: a laptop or a desktop computer?
- What do you mostly use it for? (word-processing, graphics, email, games...)
- How much time do you spend on the Internet each day?
- What do you generally use the Internet for? (playing games, email, research...)
- How do you prefer to stay in touch with your friends and family? (face-to-face communication, landline telephone, mobile phone, email, letters...)

2 Match the words in Column A with the definitions in Column B. One has been done for you as an example.

A	B
a. keyboarding → iii	i. information
b. memory	ii. save
c. display	iii. typing
d. user-friendly	iv. show on the screen
e. laptop	v. ultra-modern
f. scroll	vi. small portable computer
g. data	vii. move up or down
h. store	viii. information storage facility
i. cutting-edge	ix. well-designed and easy to use

VOCABULARY

Vocabulary Bank

Nouns & Noun Phrases	Verbs	Adjectives
appliance	to log on/off	advanced
blog	to allow	hi-tech
browser	to enable	modern
cable	to close	up-to-date
cursor	to open	state-of-the-art
cyber space	to highlight	cutting-edge
data	to scroll up/down	leading-edge
default setting	to copy	user-friendly
desktop	to cut	dial-up
device	to paste	broadband
document	to print	
email	to save	
file	to double-click	
flash drive / memory stick	to download	
folder	to upload	
font	to crash	
function	to connect	
gadget	to delete	
hardware	to edit	
icon	to exit	
Internet	to display	
IT (information technology)	to operate	
keyboard	to hack (into)	
laptop		
memory		
microchip		
modem		
monitor		
mouse		
network		
password		
PC (personal computer)		
printer		
scanner		
silicon chip		
software		
the digital age		
username		
website		
word-processing		
word-processor		
World Wide Web		

Collocations

to connect to the Internet
to access a database
to send a message
to click (on)
to store information
to download information from
to upload information (on)to
a wireless connection

the virtual world (of the Internet)
to surf the (Inter)net
to play computer games
to play/work on the computer

'allow' and 'enable'

someone or something **allows** someone or something **to do** something
someone or something **enables** someone or something **to do** something

If A **allows** B to happen, A creates the opportunity for B to happen.
If A **enables** B **to** happen, A gives B the opportunity to do something or makes it possible.

3 *With a partner, take turns making sentences by joining phrases from column (a) to phrases from column (b) using the verbs* ***allow*** *or* ***enable****. They are interchangeable.*

For example:

A modem **enables** you **to** connect to the Internet.
A modem **allows** you **to** connect to the Internet.

(a)		(b)
a. A modem		surf the web
b. A word-processor		take photos
c. A flash-drive		type documents
d. A wireless connection		listen to music
e. Email		download information
f. A printer	**allows** you **to**	store information
g. A browser		record sound
h. A search engine	*or*	connect to the Internet
i. An instant messenger	**enables** you **to**	send and receive messages
j. A microphone		chat with/to friends
k. Speakers		access a website
l. A digital camera		print a document
		connect to the Internet without a modem
		search for information on the Internet

Paraphrasing

Remember: If you cannot recall the correct word for something, you can describe it or explain it using other words.

4 *Circle 8 words below. Do not tell your partner which words you have chosen.*

word-processor	browser	website	wall socket
monitor	laptop	mouse	modem
keyboard	blog	flash-drive	database
cable			

Explain your words to your partner without saying the word itself. Your partner will guess which word you are paraphrasing.

You may find some of the following phrases helpful to introduce your paraphrases:

You know, it's a...	It's like a...
It's a kind of ...	It's a thing you use to...
It's a way of ...	It's a place where...
It's a device/gadget that	

Example: It's a device that you use to move the cursor over the page. [mouse]

Put it all together

Describe an interesting or unusual site that you have visited on the Internet.
You should say:
what it is
when you visited it
what you found out
and explain why it was interesting.

5 *Name 3 sites you have visited.*

[1] .... [2] .... [3] ....

6 *Make notes about each site.*

Site 1	Site 2	Site 3

7 *Underline the key word(s) in the first line of the prompt card. Look at your notes and choose the most* ***interesting*** *or* ***unusual*** *website of the three. Check that your notes match the prompts on the cue card. Now, talk to your partner for one to two minutes on the topic. After your talk, ask your partner to rate the interest level on a scale from 1-5. (1 = not very interesting and 5 = extremely interesting.)*

Rounding-off questions

At the end of your long turn, the examiner may ask you one or two follow-up questions before beginning Part 3 of the test. You only need to give a short answer to a follow-up question: **yes** or **no + auxiliary** verb is usually all that is necessary. Use the **same tense** the examiner uses.

For example:

Have any of your friends used this website?

- 'Yes, they **have**.'
- 'No, they **haven't**.'

8 *Underline the auxiliary verbs in the follow-up questions below. These are the verbs (and tenses) you will use in your answers.*

a. Would you recommend this site to a friend?
b. Do you enjoy surfing the net?
c. Was it hard to find this site?
d. Will you tell other people about this site?
e. Did you learn much from it?
f. Is it suitable for very young people?

9 *With a partner, ask and answer the questions above. Give short answers.*

If the rounding-off, or follow-up question is a 'wh' type question, you will have to give a full answer, but keep it brief.

For example:

'How did you find out about this website?'

- 'Oh, I just found it when I was surfing the net one day.'
- 'My classmate told me about it.'

10 *Now ask and answer the following questions:*

a. What kind of person would find this website useful?
b. How often do you try a new website?
c. Why did you go to this website in particular?

Focus on Part 3 of the IELTS Speaking Test

PRONUNCIATION

In the IELTS Speaking Test, the examiner will be listening for grouping of information and ideas. To get a good pronunciation mark, it is important that you can do this. If you pronounce each word separately, or stop in the middle of phrases, you may get a poor score.

In English, we use linking, pauses and pitch changes to mark groups of information.

linking = joining words together in one smooth flow
pauses = brief stops
pitch = the way the voice moves up or down

Generally, it is true that at the end of each group of information, if the voice goes up or stays level, it signals that the information is unfinished; the speaker is going to add more. If the pitch of the voice goes down, it signals the end of the statement; the information is finished.

11 Look at this Part 3 response in the box and mark the pauses between groups of information with / .

For example:

'If people in developing countries / had access to the Internet / it would be great. / They would find weather forecasts very helpful / because they would know / whether it would be safe / to go out fishing / for example / or / whether to plant their crops / or harvest them / or ...'

> ...whether they should do something else. They could check prices for their produce so they would know whether the buyer was offering them a fair price. Another thing that would be really useful would be all kinds of information such as medical advice and farming advice of course but I suppose the most important thing would be access to education. You know children and not just children in remote villages could have school lessons. Also if poor people in the countryside needed to move to town to find work they would be able to check on jobs in the nearest town.

12 Listen to the audio recording and check. Sometimes pauses are very short, and sometimes they are longer. You can mark longer pauses with //.

13 Listen to the audio recording of a practice Part 3 of the Speaking Test. Focus on the way the speakers group information together and pause between phrases. Pay attention to stress and pitch, too. You can mark these on the transcript at the end of the unit.

GRAMMAR

14 Look at the following Part 3 question.

'If poor people in developing countries had access to the Internet, what kinds of information would be most helpful or of most interest to them?'

The **second conditional** is used for situations that are are imagined, not real.

If + past (unreal situation)		**+ would** (result)	+ base form verb
	or	**+ could** (= would be able to)	+ base form verb

For example:

If poor people had access to the Internet (but they don't), they would find weather forecasts most helpful.

If ...	they would be able to look for work.
If ...	they could check price.
If ...	they would get farming advice.
If ...	they could get medical advice.
If ...	they could get education information.

15 Complete the statements below using the second conditional.

a. If they checked weather forecasts, they...
b. If they searched the job websites, ...
c. If they checked agricultural prices, ...
d. If they received farming advice,...
e. If they got medical advice, ...
f. If they had access to education information, ...

16 Work with a partner. Take turns saying your completed sentences.

FLUENCY AND COHERENCE

17 Work with a partner. Student A asks the Part 3 questions and Student B answers them with book closed. Take turns. You may use ideas from the recorded discussion but do not memorise complete answers. Remember:

- *Pause only between groups of information.*
- *Use pitch to signal finished and unfinished information.*
- *Stress important words.*
- *Paraphrase if you cannot recall a word.*

A. 'Well, you've talked about a particular website and now I'd like to ask you a few more general questions. Let's begin by talking about communication technology...Can you tell me how modern communication technology has changed people's lives?'
B. ...
A. 'Yes, it's instantaneous, but do you think communication technology has had any negative impact on the quality of people's lives?'
B. ...
A. 'Some people say our lives are dominated by computers. Do you agree?'
B. ...
A. 'So, would you say society is safer because of communication technology?'
B. ...
A. 'What do you mean?'
B. ...
A. 'Do you think older people have a different attitude towards new technology?'
B. ...

A. 'Let's talk about technology in the developing world. How can communication technology, such as the Internet, help people in developing countries?'

B. ...

A. 'If poor people in developing countries had access to the Internet in their language, what kinds of information would be most helpful or of most interest to them?'

B. ...

TRANSCRIPT:

'Well, you've talked about a particular website and now I'd like to ask you a few more general questions. Let's begin by talking about communication technology...Can you tell me how modern communication technology has changed people's lives?'

'Well, I think in many ways it has made our lives easier. Everything is so convenient ... and communication nowadays is so ins... instant..., you know, it happens immediately. We can contact our friends and family, do our business and...banking at any time of the day or night...in any part of the world.'

'Yes, it's instantaneous, but do you think communication technology has had any negative impact on the quality of people's lives?'

'Negative impact, mmm, well, actually it has probably had a negative impact on our privacy. There are always interruptions in our lives. Someone is always texting or the phone is ringing. You can' t get away from it. And mobile phones these days can take your picture and you don't know that someone has got your picture. There's a lot of Internet addiction too. Young people especially, play on the computer for hours and hours and they forget how to socialise.'

'Some people say our lives are dominated by computers. Do you agree?'

'Oh, definitely. Computers are everywhere in our lives—at home, at work, in factories, in the shops—nearly everything has a microchip in it these days. Yes, to some extent, computers control our lives.'

'So, would you say society is safer because of communication technology?'

'Yes and no. In lots of ways, society is safer. If I am lost or in trouble, I can get help immediately if I have my mobile phone with me. But, some people, well, they don't use technology in a good way.'

'What do you mean?'

'There are some people who use the Internet for really bad things, like... hacking... and criminals. Criminals use technology too. I guess, in some ways, technology makes crime easier. On the other hand, police can use technology to catch them, too.'

'Do you think older people have a different attitude towards new technology?'

'Mmm. Yes. Older people don't usually like new technology. They think it is difficult to use.'

' Let's talk about technology in the developing world. How can communication technology, such as the Internet, help people in developing countries?'

'That's a good question. If it is in their language, it will help them a lot. It can give them new ideas; they can learn new skills and get a lot of good information.'

'If poor people in developing countries had access to the Internet in their language, what kinds of information would be most helpful or of most interest to them?'

'Firstly, I think they would find weather forecasts most helpful. If they checked the weather forecast, they could find out the best time to go fishing, or plant their crops, or harvest them. Secondly, if they needed to leave their village to find work, they could check job websites to find out the nearest town with available work. Actually, there are many things that could help them... They could get farming advice, medical advice... and... education. Education is probably the most helpful and the most important.'

UNIT 20 Tourism

Focus on Part 1 of the IELTS Speaking Test

WARM-UP

A

B

C

D

1 Look at each photograph and discuss these questions with a partner.

a. Where do you think it is?
b. What kinds of people (or animals) live there?
c. What would it be like to live there?
d. Would you like to live there? Why / Why not?
e. Would you like to visit as a tourist? Why / Why not?

2 *Think about this question:*

If you could go anywhere, where in the world would you like to go?

3 *Tell your partner and give reasons for your choice.*

4 *With your partner, consider the possible effects of tourism on these places in the photographs. Make notes on the chart. The first one has been done for you.*

Place	Positive	Negative
A	Growth in eco-tourism Economic benefits Money to use for research Increased awareness of global warming etc Understanding of endangered animals	Pollution Damage to environment Changes to animals' natural habitat
B		
C		
D		

5 *Work with a different partner this time. Ask your partner what the positive and negative effects of tourism might be on the four places. If your new partner has different ideas, add more notes to your chart.*

VOCABULARY

There are many different ways to talk about the good and bad side of things. Study the table below.

(adjective)	+	–
financial economic social socioeconomic environmental cultural human	pro(s) advantage(s) benefit(s) [positive] effect(s) [positive] impact(s)	con(s) disadvantage(s) drawback(s) problem(s) cost(s) risk(s) danger(s) [negative] effect(s) [negative] impact(s)

For example:

a financial advantage
a social drawback
the human impact
} *of tourism*

Note the word order of adjectives before nouns: **opinions** often come before **descriptions**.

For example:

a negative environmental *effect*
a positive cultural *benefit*

When we compare the pros and cons of any particular idea, we often use the verb **outweigh**. If A **outweighs** B, A is more important or of greater benefit than B.

For example:

The socioeconomic advantages ***outweigh*** *the environmental drawbacks.*

We often use the adverb **far** for emphasis.

For example:

The cultural benefits ***far outweigh*** *the financial costs.*

6 *Look back at your chart of the four tourist destinations, A, B, C, D. Use your notes on that chart, together with the table above, to make new sentences about the four places.*

7 *Now, while only looking at the photographs on the first page of this unit, practise with a partner talking about the positive and negative effects of tourism on each place.*

Vocabulary Bank

Nouns

history
geography
climate
scenery
lifestyle
resources
development
impact
environment
culture
economy
policy
respect
aim
goal
objective
tax
tariff
administration
regulation(s)
requirement
impression

Verbs

to regulate
to restrict

Adjectives

coastal
rural
urban

mountainous
world-wide
(un)controlled
devastating
sustainable
socioeconomic

Collocations

the tourism industry
tourist operators
a tourism policy
tourist guide
adventure tourism
eco-tourism
exchange rate

a manageable level of development
a lack of infrastructure

the developing world
the developed world

to promote understanding
growth and development
problems associated with...

travel by air / by plane
by rail / by train
by road / by car/bus/bicycle
by sea / by boat
on foot

environmentally friendly
ecologically friendly
socially acceptable
culturally acceptable
economically viable

8 Tick √ the words in the Vocabulary Bank that you know. Use a dictionary to help you with the meanings of new words and phrases.

9 Listen to the audio recording. Mark stressed syllables and repeat the words several times.

10 Without looking at the Vocabulary Bank, see how many words and phrases you can remember. Write them in your notebook.

11 Look at the cue card and use the prompts to make notes below.

Describe a city or town that you have visited.

You should say:

where it is

how you got there

what there is to do in that city or town

and explain why you went there.

City/town: ____________________

Where? ____________________

Travelled by: ____________________

You can do / go / see: ____________________

____

____

Went there to: ____________________

Because: ____________________

____

12 *Look back at your notes and try to think of more details to expand on each prompt.*

a. What more can you say about the town and its location?
b. Describe the bus/train/car/boat/plane journey in detail (the weather, the people etc).
c. Think of all the things visitors can do or see there, and where they can go. (You may have gone there to visit someone or do something in particular. This prompt, however, is asking you to talk about whatever is possible or available. It's okay to describe quite ordinary things. Your objective is to keep talking for two minutes.)
d. You've probably already given the main reason or purpose behind your visit. Was there a secondary reason perhaps, anything you can add?

13 *Look at the verb tenses in the prompts. Notice what tense you can use to describe the location of the town and what there is to do there. Notice what tense you should use to describe the journey and the purpose or reason for your visit.*

14 *Now, talk to your partner for two minutes on this topic. Your partner will time you. If you stop before the time is up, your partner should remain silent and give you the opportunity to say more. As soon as you reach the two-minute limit, your partner should say: "Thank you". That is the signal for you to finish. You must stop then.*

The Examiner cannot let you talk for longer than two minutes in this part of the test.

15 *Finish with a rounding-off question. Choose one from the examples below or make up a suitable question of your own.*

For example:

Do you think you'll visit this town/city again?

Would you recommend this town/city as a good place to visit?

PRONUNCIATION

Rhythm, in English, is the **pattern of strong and weak stress**.

The strong stresses have about the same timing between them. (If we think in terms of music, they are the beat.)

We pronounce the weak stresses in the **time between** the strong stresses. It does not matter how many weak stresses are between the strong stresses.

Remember, the strong stresses are **information** words and the weak stresses are usually **grammar** words.

Speaking with English Rhythm

- pronounce the weak words shorter
- use the schwa /ə/
- use contractions
- link words together
- pronounce the stressed (information) words longer & louder

If there are no (or very few) weak words between the stressed words (or beats), the stressed words are made longer.

16 Listen to the audio recording.

Tap your finger on your desk when you hear the stressed words.

	/	/	/	/
a. The	city I've	visited is	Tokyo.	
b. I	went to	Tokyo, which is the	capital of	Japan,
with my	family	last	year.	
c. My	uncle	drove us to the	airport	
on a very	hot	summer's	day.	

17 Read along with the audio recording.

English is a stress-timed language so this beat, or rhythm, is very important. If you say all the words with equal stress, English speakers will have difficulty understanding you. In fact, you may sound unfriendly, rude or angry. The Examiner listens for natural English rhythm.

18 *Look back at your notes for the Part 2 prompt card. In your notebook, write out some full sentences of things you'd like to say.*

19 *Now, think about English rhythm:*

- Mark the strong beats (the stressed syllables of the stressed information words).
- Mark the linking between the words.
- Think about using the schwa in the weak words.
- Make contractions where possible.

20 *Say each sentence with one breath, keeping your voice going and pausing only at the end of information groups or sentences.*

Focus on Part 3 of the IELTS Speaking Test

GRAMMAR

In response to most questions in Part 3, you will give an **opinion**.

There are several ways to begin your answer. These are not the only ways and it is possible to answer directly without using one of these opening phrases. However, an opening phrase sounds more natural and gives you a little more thinking time.

21 *Put these phrases into the appropriate boxes below.*

To my mind	As far as I'm concerned	I believe in
I don't believe	I'm against	I'm not sure
I don't think	I'm in favour of	In my opinion
In my view	Personally, I think	Possibly, but
I have my doubts about		

Positive (agree)	Neutral	Negative (disagree or want to give alternative)

When we **give an opinion** or **suggest a solution**, we can use **should**.

For example:

The government should promote eco-tourism.

We often use **should** with **I think** or **I don't think**.

For example:

I don't think the government should allow tourism in sensitive areas.

We sometimes use **ought to** instead of should.

For example:

The government ought to promote eco-tourism.

FLUENCY AND COHERENCE

22 *Listen to one candidate's response to a question in Part 3 of the Speaking Test about the negative impact of tourism.*

Examiner: 'Now, let's discuss more general ideas about tourism. Let's start with tourism and the environment. Can you tell me about any negative impact that tourism can have on the natural environment?'

Candidate: 'Okay, negative impact. Mmm. Firstly, if we think about how the tourists get to their destination... They have to travel by plane, boat, bus, train or car—and every kind of transport produces air pollution and noise pollution. Then, there is the problem of resources. Tourists use lots of resources like energy, food and specially water. I think visitors, especially westerners, use lots more water than the local population. The tourist facilities, you know, the infrastructure they need, like hotels and roads, results in forest being cut down or the habitat of animals being destroyed. Tourists make a lot of rubbish, also. And if they go to look at animals, the animals can be disturbed by the noise and their habitat might be damaged. Tourists often walk on plants and damage them; they sometimes take plants too, or bits of coral from under the sea, as souvenirs—and in this way they destroy the environment.'

23 *Listen to the examiner's next question:*

'So, what should tourists, or governments, or even individuals, do to minimise or solve these problems?'

24 *Answer the question by completing the sentences giving your opinion and suggesting solutions.*

a. I think the government should ....

b. I don't think people ought to ....

c. In my view, tourists should ....

d. I really believe tourist operators ought to ....

e. As far as I'm concerned, we ought to ....

f. Personally, I think ....

25 *Work with a partner, taking turns to make your suggestions.*

Answer Key

Unit 1 Education

1. [*Audio*

a. I'm an English student.
b. I'm studying at New Oriental Foreign Language School.
c. I need to improve my English.
d. I want to take the IELTS exam.
e. It's a lot of fun! Or: It's an important language to learn.
f. I come from Beijing.]

2. [*Audio*

a. What's your first name?
b. What's your family name?
c. Where do you come from?
d. Are you a student or do you have a job?
e. Why are you studying English?
f. Where are you studying English?
g. What do you enjoy about studying English?]

3. Pair work— many possible answers

4. Dictionary work

5. Some possible answers:
Example: a. What subjects are compulsory in your school?
Maths / language / history /
b. Maths, physics, chemistry, history, sports, languages
c. Maths, physics, chemistry, history, sports, languages
d. Naughty, strict, hit, corporal, punishment, detention, rules, uniform
e. Test, primary, secondary
f. Assignments, marks, optional, compulsory

6. [*Audio*

subject	*public*	*sports*	*rules*
class	*discipline*	*library*	*uniform*
physics	*homework*	*language*	*gymnasium*
chemistry	*assignments*	*history*	*laboratory*
maths	*test*	*culture*	*absent*
compulsory	*marks*	*strict*	*attendance*
optional	*exams*	*hit*	*junior*
co-ed	*primary*	*corporal*	*senior*
single sex	*secondary*	*punishment*	*science*
private	*naughty*	*detention*	*major*]

7.

1 syllable	2 syllables	3 or more syllables
hit	public	optional
class	subject	chemistry
maths	physics	compulsory
test	co-ed	single sex
marks	private	discipline
sports	homework	assignments
strict	exams	primary
rules	naughty	secondary
	language	library
	culture	history
	major	corporal
	science	punishment
		detention
		uniform
		senior
		junior

8. *Answers and* [*Audio*

a. What subjects are compulsory in your school?
In my school we have to take language and maths but we can choose history or chemistry.
b. What are your favourite subjects?
I really like English because it's so interesting and the teacher is so funny!
c. What subjects do you not like?
I hate maths because it's boring and it's too hard.
d. Tell me about discipline in your school.
Our school is very strict. There are lots of rules. You have to wear a uniform and you can't talk in class.
e. What exams do you take?
At the end of Senior High everyone takes the University Entrance exam. It's really difficult and we have to do a lot of work.
f. How much homework do you have?
Lots! I have to work every night and I get so tired!]

9. Pair work

10. Individual work

11. Group work
a. Example for students
I ~~am~~ come from a small town in Hunan Province, China.
I come from a small town in Hunan Province, China.
b. I don't like learning history because it is not useful to me.
c. I don't like studying biology as it is so difficult for me to understand science.
d. I like studying English because it's an important language to learn.
e. I really like studying maths because I want to be a maths teacher.

13. Pair work

14. a) Yes, the student liked the teacher.
b) She liked her because she was kind, helpful and patient and gave the children sweets.
[*Audio*
I remember a teacher I had at primary school who was wonderful. From the first day she was friendly and kind towards the students who were 8 years old. But she was also strict. I mean on the first day she took out this old fashioned strap and banged it on the desk and we all got such a fright, but she was just trying to show us she was in control. She wasn't really that scary although she was quite short and she spoke in a loud voice. Everybody called her Mrs. T. She taught us for every subject, so she taught us English, maths, writing, and actually I can't

remember what else! I guess what I used to enjoy most about her classes was her personality and the fact that she cared about all of her students, even the naughty ones. I remember her daughter lived in America and she used to send over American sweets and chewing gum for Mrs. T to give to the good students. All the students tried to be really good to get that reward! I particularly remember my teacher, Mrs. T, because she was so kind, helpful and patient. I was very young and she was like a mother to me, gentle but strict at the same time.]

15.

Different Parts of the Talk:	**Short Notes:**
§1: What the teacher was like (personality and appearance)	Wonderful, friendly, kind Strict—strap, short, loud voice Mrs T
§2: What subjects she taught	Taught every subject.
§3: What the speaker enjoyed about her classes	Her personality Cared for everyone American sweets
§4: Why the speaker remembered her	Kind, helpful, patient Like a mother

16. a. No b. Yes c. No

17-18. Individual notes

19. Timed practice

Unit 2 Food

1. Possible answers:
Healthy Food: *apple, rice, banana, tomato, noodles, chicken, bread, cabbage, dumpling, egg, salad, potato, lettuce, sandwich, celery, cheese, pasta, spinach, sushi*
Junk Food: *hamburger, KFC, hotdog, biscuits, cake, chips, cheeseburger, pizza, ice cream, chocolate, meat pie*

2. [*Audio*

Apple	*Dumpling*	*Pasta*	*Chips*
Rice	*Egg*	*Spinach*	*Cheeseburger*
Banana	*Salad*	*Suchi*	*Pizza*
Tomato	*Potato*	*Hamburger*	*Ice cream*
Noodles	*Lettuce*	*KFC*	*Chocolate*
Chicken	*Sandwich*	*Hotdog*	*Meat Pie*]
Bread	*Celery*	*Biscuits*	
Cabbage	*Cheese*	*Cake*	

3. [*Audio*
Speaker 1: *My family and I always do our food shopping at the local markets because all the fruit and vegetables are so fresh.*
Speaker 2: *I really like fast food, and my favourite is pizza—yummy!*
Speaker 3: *I never cook because I don't know how! My parents always cook for me.*
Speaker 4: *I prefer eating in restaurants to eating at home, because you don't have to do the dishes afterwards!*
Speaker 5: *We usually eat toast or cereal with fruit for breakfast and on the weekend we might go out for bacon and eggs.*]

4. [*Audio*
a. I never cook because I don't know how.
b. I really like fast food.
c. I prefer eating in restaurants to eating at home.
d. My favourite food is pizza.
e. We usually eat toast or cereal for breakfast.]

5. i. Example:
What's your favourite food?→ d. My favourite food is pizza.
ii. I never cook because I don't know how.
iii. I prefer eating in restaurants to eating at home.
iv. We usually eat toast or cereal for breakfast.
v. I really like fast food.

6. Answers and [*Audio*
a. Tell me about your favourite food?
b. Do you like to cook?
c. Do you prefer to eat out or eat at home?
d. What do you usually eat for breakfast?
e. Do you like fast food?]

7. Listen and repeat

8. Pair work

9. Soup / hotdog / taste / pizza hut / donut / sweet snack / overweight / soft drink / chocolate / big mac / carrot / breakfast / chip / chicken nugget / diet / fast / milk / weight / eat

10. [*Audio*
Soup / hotdog / taste / pizza hut / donut / sweet snack / overweight / softdrink / chocolate / big mac / carrot / breakfast / chip / chicken nugget / diet / fast / milk / weight / eat]
Answers

/p/ ending	/t/ ending	/k/ ending
soup chip	taste pizza hut sweet fat soft chocolate carrot breakfast chicken nugget diet fast weight eat	snack sweet snack drink big Mac milk hotdog (*this has /g/ ending*)

11. Listen and repeat

12. [*Audio*
a. A soft drink is unhealthy because it contains a lot of sugar.
b. Pizza Hut is a worldwide fast food restaurant.
c. If you want to lose weight, you shouldn't eat too much junk food.
d. A balanced diet is an important part of keeping healthy.
e. He eats a hotdog every day.

f. *Chocolate milk is very tasty.*
g. *People often eat dumplings for breakfast in China.*
h. *I eat a carrot every day as part of a healthy diet.*
i. *Bananas are the perfect fruit.*
j. *He ate too many Big Macs and now he is overweight.*]

13. Answers and [*Audio*
a. *Soft drinks are not very healthy.*
b. *Pizza Hut is a fast food restaurant.*
c. *It's important to eat healthy food.*
d. *He likes to eat a hotdog for lunch.*]

14. Listen and repeat

15. Practice

16. [*Audio*
Pardon
Could you repeat that please?
Sorry?
Sorry, I didn't hear you. Could you repeat the question?]

17-22 Pairwork—examples—individual practice

23. a. healthier　　e. greasier
b. tastier　　f. spicier
c. sweeter　　g. more delicious
d. oilier/more oily　　h. yummier

24. a. +　　e. -
b. +　　f. + (or-depending on individual taste)
c. +　　g. +
d. -　　h. +

25-27. Pair work and individual practice

28. [*Audio*
I'm going to talk about a meal I enjoyed. It was right after my university graduation, when I was about 21. My whole family came to see me graduate and it was a very proud day. After the ceremony we all went to a nearby restaurant, which was busy with other families who were all doing the same thing. The atmosphere was exciting and busy. The restaurant was beautiful, with long tables, candles and flowers. My family also gave me a huge bunch of flowers and some cards and special gifts. I was there with my mum, dad, two brothers and my grandfather and I remember that we ordered a lot of seafood and champagne to celebrate. I can't really remember what else we ate, but the seafood was delicious. Oh, that's right, we had lobster to share, which was amazing. We spent all afternoon at the restaurant, talking, eating and laughing. And of course, we took lots of photos. My father made a speech of congratulations and wished me good luck for the future. It was such an enjoyable day because I knew that my family was very proud of me and we all shared my celebration together. And everything about the restaurant was perfect. The waiters were friendly and the food was fantastic. I am happy that I remember this special day in my life so clearly.]

29. a. Seafood/lobster/champagne
b. It was a celebration and her family were proud of her. / Everything was perfect.

30. Present simple in *italics*; past tense <u>underlined</u>.
I'm going to talk about a meal I <u>enjoyed</u>. It <u>was</u> right after my university graduation, when I <u>was</u> about 21. My whole family <u>came</u> to see me graduate and it <u>was</u> a very proud day. After the ceremony we all <u>went</u> to a nearby restaurant, which <u>was</u> busy with other families who <u>were</u> all doing the same thing. The atmosphere <u>was</u> exciting and busy. The restaurant <u>was</u> beautiful, with long tables, candles and flowers. My family also <u>gave</u> me a huge bunch of flowers and some cards and special gifts. I <u>was</u> there with my mum, dad, two brothers and my grandfather and I ***remember*** that we <u>ordered</u> a lot of seafood and champagne to celebrate. I can't really ***remember*** what else we <u>ate</u>, but the seafood <u>was</u> delicious. Oh, that's right; we <u>had</u> lobster to share, which <u>was</u> amazing. We <u>spent</u> all afternoon at the restaurant, talking, eating and laughing. And of course, we <u>took</u> heaps of photos. My father <u>made</u> a speech of congratulations and <u>wished</u> me good luck for the future. It <u>was</u> such an enjoyable day because I <u>knew</u> that my family <u>was</u> very proud of me and we all <u>shared</u> my celebration together. And everything about the restaurant <u>was</u> perfect. The waiters <u>were</u> friendly and the food <u>was</u> fantastic. I ***am*** happy that I ***remember*** this special day in my life so clearly.
The speaker mainly uses past simple verbs. Past simple was also used in the prompt card.

31-33. Individual and Pairwork

Unit 3　Sport and Exercise

1. [*Audio*
a. *I play basketball with my friends every day after school.*
b. *I'm not very good at soccer, but I love it.*
c. *In my free time, I often like watching tennis matches on television.*
d. *I don't watch rugby very much because it's not very popular in China.*
e. *On the weekends, I play table tennis with my dad.*]

2. Individual work—many possible answers

3. Individual work

4.

DO	PLAY	GO
athletics gymnastics weight Lifting	football hockey soccer rugby volleyball table tennis golf American football basketball tennis badminton snooker	swimming cycling skiing snowboarding skating kayaking surfing boxing (also 'DO') motor racing (also 'DO') show jumping sailing

5. Individual answers

6. Pair work— practice

7. a. Do you prefer to exercise alone or with friends?
b. Do you like to go swimming in the sea?
c. How often do you go running?
d. Do you exercise regularly?
e. Do you think exercise is important?

8. [*Audio*
a. Do you prefer to exercise alone or with friends?
b. Do you like to go swimming in the sea?
c. How often do you go running?
d. Do you exercise regularly?
e. Do you think exercise is important?]

9. Listen and repeat

10. Pair work—practice

11. Individual answers

12. Pair work—practice

13. [*Audio*

Very	*Win*	*Various*
Wetsuit	*Caving*	*Week*
Television	*Diving*	*Walk*]
Volleyball	*Weightlifting*	

Answers:

/v/	/w/
very television volleyball caving diving various	wetsuit win weight lifting week walk

14. Listen and repeat

15.

never	not very often		quite a lot	a lot	all the time
hardly ever	not very much	sometimes	quite often	often	always

16. a. Example for students
A: Do you go swimming at the pool very often?
B: Yes, quite a lot. It relaxes me.
b. B: Never! I hate it.
c. B: Well, I try to go quite often / often, but sometimes I just feel like sleeping instead!
d. B: Hardly ever / Never. I always forget my homework.

17. [*Audio*
A: Do you go swimming at the pool very often?
B: Yes, quite a lot. It relaxes me.
A: Do you watch football on television much?
B: Never! I hate it.
A: How often do you go jogging?
B: Well, I try to go quite often, but sometimes I just feel like sleeping instead!
A: Do you study English much at home?
B: Hardly ever. I always forget my homework.]

18. Listen and repeat

19. a. Example for students
I play soccer quite a lot because I like it.
b. Do you often play table tennis?
c. My dad sometimes watches soccer on television with me.
OR: Sometimes my dad watches soccer on television with me.
OR: My dad watches soccer on television with me sometimes.
Note: 'Sometimes' can go at the beginning, middle and end.
d. I don't watch sport on television very much.
e. My mum comes to watch my tennis matches quite a lot.
f. I always go swimming at the pool because I like it.

20. Pair work

21. Speaker 1: Prompt card 1
Speaker 2: Prompt card 2
[*Audio*
Speaker 1: *Okay, I'm going to speak about a sport that I enjoy playing: basketball. To play basketball, you need a ball, a court, and two hoops at either end. Of course, you also need players—five on each side. The aim of the game is to get the ball through the hoop at each end. Players do this by dribbling the basketball down the court and passing it to other players to move the ball in the right direction. Meanwhile, the members of the other team try to stop them from doing this. They can try to stop them by guarding them very closely and trying to get the ball from them. Basketball is played in four quarters, and players can be swapped during this time. It takes about an hour but that depends on how often the referee stops them. In my team, I play centre and so I have to run around a lot and help move the basketball down the court. I'm also pretty good at shooting, so I get lots of chances to score points. I guess I like playing basketball because of the way it makes me feel. I feel quite excited when I play and it also feels good to be part of a team, especially when we're winning!*]

Speaker 2: *A sport that I'd like to try is white water rafting. I guess it's more of an extreme sport really. I've always been keen to try it, ever since I saw a programme on television which showed people rafting on this huge river in South America somewhere. It looked amazing, but scary at the same time. To do white water rafting, I think you need to go with a company who organises it all for you, because you need a lot of stuff: lifejackets, helmets, wetsuits and all that kind of thing. The boats they use are inflatable rafts, and you are given little paddles to row with. From what I saw, you start off at the top of a river and float down until you get to a type of small waterfall, where the water is moving very fast, and the raft goes over and down to the next part of the river. That's when it gets exciting! I saw people falling out and going under the water, but they all looked like they were having a great time. I'd love to try it because it looks so exciting and a little bit dangerous at the same time, so I think it'd be quite thrilling. And I love swimming so hopefully I'd be Okay!*]

22-23. Individual work

24-25. Pair work

Unit 4 Media

1-3. Pair work

4. [*Audio*

chat show	*educational*	*it was terrified*
sports programme	*old fashioned*	*it was terrifying*
documentary	*modern*	*it was scared*
music programme	*scary*	*it was scary*
horror movie	*terrifying*	*it was amused*
quiz	*interesting*	*it was amusing*
comedy	*fascinating*	*it's a true story*
romance	*funny*	*it's based on fact*
action movie	*amusing*	*it's partly true*
autobiography	*humorous*	*it's fiction*
biography	*exciting*	*it got my attention*
historical movie	*boring*	*good looking actor*
fiction	*relaxing*	*good looking actress*]
science fiction	*popular*	
martial arts	*famous*	
drama		
crime		
cartoon		
fantasy		
news		
current affairs		
weather report		
musical		
western		
thriller		

5. Listen and repeat

6. On the audio, the Chant is read through once at normal speed. The second time one line is read at a time followed by a pause. This gives the students the opportunity to repeat after each line and concentrate on their pronunciation.

[*Audio*

Funny, funnier, funniest	*Scary, scarier, scariest*
The funniest show on TV	*The scariest show on TV*
*This *programme's the funniest*	*This *programme's the scariest*
The best one for you to see.	*The worst one for you to see!*]

7. Listen and repeat

[*Audio: The news is more interesting than the weather, but it isn't as interesting as a sports programme.*]

8. Listen and repeat—focus on sentence stress and linking

[*Audio:*

a. A comedy is more exciting than a documentary, but it isn't as exciting as a horror movie.

b. A quiz is more educational than the weather, but it isn't as educational as a documentary.

c. A quiz is funnier than a documentary, but it isn't as funny as a comedy.

d. A documentary is more boring than the news, but it isn't as boring as the weather.

e. A movie is more relaxing than a sports programme, but it isn't as relaxing as a music programme.

f. An action movie is scarier than the news, but it isn't as scary as a horror movie.]

9. This exercise could be a written or spoken exercise.

Possible answers:

a. Jill is shorter than Lin and Sam. She's the shortest of them all.
Lin is older than Jill, but she isn't as old as Sam.
Lin isn't as short as Jill, but she is shorter than Sam.
Sam is the oldest of them all.

b. A newspaper is as popular as a television for hearing the news.
A computer is more modern than a radio and a newspaper.
A radio is more old fashioned than a television, but a television isn't more popular than a radio.
Computers are the most modern of all media.

c. A radio can be more interesting than a newspaper, but it isn't as interesting as a television.
A television isn't as educational as a newspaper, but it is more educational than a magazine.
A television is the most interesting of them all.
A magazine is the least educational of them all.

d. An action movie is as exciting as a thriller.
A comedy is more amusing than an action movie.
A thriller is the scariest (of them all).
A comedy is the least scary.

10. Individual and pair work

11. Example

12. Individual work. Ensure the students only write in note form, not in long sentences.

Sample answer:

Question	Your notes
What was the movie called?	Raising Ned Devine
When and where did you see it?	Last year...On TV And 4 years ago at the cinema
What type of movie was it?	Comedy
Why did you enjoy it?	Unusual Main character—old, skinny, funny, lovable. Normal, everyday, village life

13. Possible answer:

[*Audio:*

A movie I have seen and enjoyed was called Raising Ned Devine. I saw it last year on television but actually that was the second time. The first time was about four years ago at the local cinema. Raising Ned Devine was a comedy set in a small village in Wales. The characters in the movie were just normal village people going about their daily lives. One of these people was a village leader. He took a main part in the movie. Another was an old, very skinny man who didn't have much confidence in himself. He worried a lot but he was very lovable.

I enjoyed the movie because it had an unusual story line and at the same time it showed normal everyday life in the village, and their relationships with each other.

The other reason it was so good was that the little old man was so lovable. Even though he was doing something that was wrong, you couldn't help wanting him to win in the end. He had an innocence about him.]

14. Individual and pair work

15. Pair work

16. Answers and [*Audio*

Examiner:

What type of activities did people do in their free time before the invention of radios, televisions and computers?

Candidate:

I think in the olden days people used to spend their free time reading or doing activities with their children. Fathers used to teach their sons to make things out of wood and mothers used to teach their daughters to sew. People probably played games too, such as chess and mah-jong.

Examiner:

Do you think this was a better way of life compared to how we live nowadays?

Candidate:

In some ways it was better. Families spent more time talking together whereas today we spend more time watching television or playing on the computer. I guess the parents taught the children in the olden days, but nowadays children learn a lot by themselves from the computer and television.

Examiner:

In 50 years time, do you think things will change much or will we be doing the same activities as now in our free time?

Candidate:

In my opinion, I believe we will change. I think people will see the benefits of spending more time talking together and less time by themselves in front of a computer or television. Maybe more electronic, educational games will be invented that need three or four people to play them, like Play Station games, and the whole family will be able to play together.]

17. used to and past simple

18. **Question 1:** ***used to***

What do you think your grandmother used to do in her free time?

Example answer: She used to sew and play mah-jong a lot.

Question 2: ***past simple***

What did you do with your free time yesterday?

Example answer: Yesterday, I read a magazine and watched television.

Question 3: ***used to***

Did your father or mother used to spend time teaching you things when you were a child?

Example answer: Yes they did. My mother used to teach me to bake cookies and my father used to show me how to ride a bicycle.

Note: The answer to question 3 can also be past simple.

Yes they did. My mother taught me to bake cookies and my father showed me how to ride a bicycle.

19. **Will** + base verb

Question 1:

Do you think you will have a good job in 15 years time?

Example answer: Yes. I think I will be a teacher or a famous musician.

Or

No. I think I will be a mother and enjoy looking after my children at home.

Question 2:

Do you think you will have children/grandchildren in 15 years time?

Example answer: Yes, I think I will have two children.

Or

Yes, I think I will have many grandchildren.

Question 3:

Do you think any member of your family will be famous?

Answer: Yes, maybe my brother will be famous. He's an excellent musician/speaker.

Or

No, probably not.

20. Pair work

21. Pair work

Unit 5 Relationships

1. Listen and repeat [*Audio*

Mother	*Father*
Grandmother	*Grandfather*
Uncle	*Aunt*
Cousin	*Brother*
	Sister]

2. Listen again and mark stress. Play previous audio again.

Mother	Father
Grandmother	Grandfather
Uncle	Aunt
Cousin	Brother
Sister	

3.

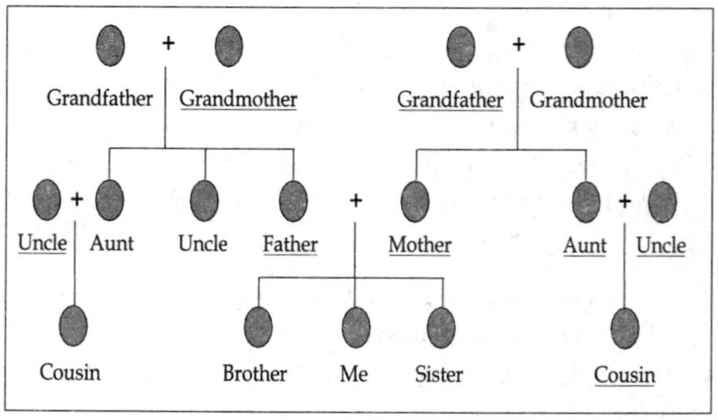

4-7. Individual and pair work

8. a. My mother's sister is my aunt.
b. My father's sister is my aunt.
c. My cousin's father is my uncle.
d. My mother's father is my grandfather.
e. My mother's sister has two children, a boy and a girl. They are my mother's niece and nephew.
f. I don't have any brothers or sisters. I am an only child.
g. My uncle and his wife don't live together any more. They are separated/divorced/.
h. Adolescence can be a difficult stage in life. You are no longer a child but not yet an adult.

i. My youngest cousin is just learning to walk. She is a toddler.

j. My aunt is divorced but she is dating again. She has a new boyfriend/partner.

9. [*Audio*

cheerful	*considerate*	*adventurous*
stubborn	*pessimistic*	*outgoing*
amusing	*sociable*	*pleasant shy*]

10.

cheerful	2 syllables
considerate	4 syllables
adventurous	4 syllables
stubborn	2 syllables
pessimistic	4 syllables
outgoing	3 syllables
amusing	3 syllables
sociable	3 syllables
pleasant	2 syllables
shy	1 syllable

11.

Cheerful	Pattern 2
Considerate	Pattern 5
Adventurous	Pattern 5
Stubborn	Pattern 2
Pessimistic	Pattern 6
Outgoing	Pattern 3

(The stress can sometimes be on the first syllable)

Amusing	Pattern 3
Sociable	Pattern 4
Pleasant	Pattern 2
Shy	Pattern 1

12. [*Audio Ex 11 & Ex 12*

Cheerful	*Considerate*
Adventurous	*Stubborn*
Pessimistic	*Outgoing*
Amusing	*Sociable*
Pleasant	*Shy*]

13. [*Audio*

I'd like to tell you about my family. I have two brothers. They're both at university. The older one is studying computer science and the younger one is studying economics. My parents are divorced. My father has remarried and lives with my stepmother and her three children, two sons and a daughter. My stepbrothers also like computers but my stepsister prefers reading books. I have a good relationship with my stepsister because we've got a lot in common. I read lots of books too and we like to discuss the ideas that we've read in them. Unfortunately, I don't get on well with my stepmother. She doesn't like me very much and we often argue. The relationship between my older brother and me is very close. We've shared many adventures together at weekends and on holidays. We play the same sports as well. The person in my family that I have the best relationship with is my mother. She's a very cheerful and considerate person and I love her very much.]

14. *I'd like to tell you about my family. I have two brothers. They're both at university. The older one is studying computer science and the younger one is studying economics. My parents are divorced. My father has remarried and lives with my stepmother and her three children, two sons and a daughter. My stepbrothers also like computers but my stepsister prefers reading books. I have a good relationship with my stepsister because we've got a lot in common. I read lots of books too and we like to discuss the ideas that we've read in them. Unfortunately, I don't get on well with my stepmother. She doesn't like me very much and we often argue. The relationship between my older brother and me is very close. We've shared many adventures together at weekends and on holidays. We play the same sports as well. The person in my family that I have the best relationship with is my mother. She's a very cheerful and considerate person and I love her very much.*

15-16. Individual work

17. Pair work—practice

18. [*Audio*

I'm going to tell you about my best friend, Lou An. We first met a few years ago at the local athletics club. She's not really good-looking or anything, but she is very helpful and thoughtful and she has a really cheerful and outgoing personality. We are about the same age and we have a lot in common so I guess that's the main reason we became friends. Of course we both love sport, especially running and cycling. She's very competitive, much more competitive than I am. She exercises for an hour or two every day. We also have similar tastes in movies and television programmes. She loves romantic comedies and so do I. She probably watches more sport on television than I do, though. When we are together we mostly spend our time playing sport, obviously, or shopping for clothes. When we go to the shopping mall, we often don't buy anything but it's fun just looking at the different styles of the new clothes and trying them on. It's good to have a reliable friend with you who will give you her honest opinion. Sometimes we go to the beach or the swimming pool together although neither of us can swim very well. Nowadays, we both seem to be very busy but we still meet at least once a week for a chat, usually on Friday afternoons. We generally go to a cafe and have something to drink. It's funny, though, our tastes are quite different in this case. Whereas I prefer coffee, she never drinks coffee. She only drinks tea.]

19. I'm going to tell you about my best friend, Lou An. We first met a few years ago at the local athletics club. She's not really good-looking or anything, but she is very helpful and thoughtful and she has a really cheerful and outgoing personality. We are about the same age and we have a lot in common so I guess that's the main reason we became friends. Of course we both love sport, especially running and cycling. She's very competitive, much more competitive than I am. She exercises for an hour or two every day. We also have similar tastes in movies and television programmes. She loves romantic comedies and so do I. She probably watches more sport on television than I do, though. When we are together we mostly spend our time playing sport, obviously, or shopping for clothes. When we go to the shopping mall, we often don't buy anything but it's fun just looking at the different styles of the new clothes and trying them on. It's good to have a reliable friend with you who will give you her honest opinion. Sometimes we go to the beach or the swimming pool together although neither of us can swim very well.

Nowadays, we both seem to be very busy but we still meet at least once a week for a chat, usually on Friday afternoons. We generally go to a cafe and have something to drink. It's funny, though, our tastes are quite different in this case. Whereas I prefer coffee, she never drinks coffee. She only drinks tea.

20. a. He enjoys unusual and rather dangerous activities like white-water rafting. He's so adventurous.
b. He's also very brave. If he hurts himself, he never complains about the pain.
c. They gave a lot of money to the earthquake victims. They're generous.
d. IELTS examiners are very patient. They are quite calm even if they have to repeat the same question three times.
e. My father is very reliable/trustworthy. When he says he'll do something, he always does it.
f. My aunt has lots of fun at parties because she is so outgoing and sociable.
g. A good friend should be honest/trustworthy and always tell the truth.
h. My youngest cousin isn't very good at talking to new people. She's quite shy.
i. Their mother is thoughtful/considerate and kind/supportive. She's a helpful person who understands other people's needs and problems.

21. Pair work—practice

22. [*Audio*
Well, I think...
I think there are a number of qualities...
Definitely, because...
Well, the main advantage...
Well, it depends on...]

23. Listen again to the audio and repeat.

24. Individual / Pair work

25. [*Audio*
Well, you've been talking about a special friend, and now I'd like to go on to talk with you some more about relationships in general. First of all, let's talk about friendship in general. How important is it for people to have friends?

***Well, I think** having friends is extremely important because everyone needs someone to talk to about their problems; not only that, but we need people to share the good times with as well. I can't imagine how lonely it would be if we didn't have any friends.*

What personal qualities do you think a real friend should have?

***I think there are a number of qualities** that a real friend has. Firstly, friends should be honest and trustworthy because you tell them your secrets and personal details, you know, really private stuff. You have to be able to trust them. Secondly, I think they should be reliable. They should meet you when they say they're going to and not let you down. I also think friends should be caring and supportive so they listen to you when you tell them your troubles and so they help you if you need help. I guess it's also more fun if they are cheerful and amusing.*

Would you say that friends are more important than family?

***Definitely, because** we spend more time with friends and they can have a huge influence on us. Sometimes that can be a bad influence, so we need to choose our friends carefully.*

Now let's move on to talk about how people form relationships. Nowadays more and more people are starting relationships on the Internet. What are the advantages of forming a relationship in this way?

***Well, the main advantage is** that starting a relationship on the Internet is so easy. Even if you are a really shy person, and not very sociable, you can still find friends on the Internet. I think some people find it much, much easier than face to face talking.*

What are the dangers?

***It seems to me that** Internet relationships are not really dangerous unless you agree to meet the person and that person has been dishonest, you know, pretending to be someone else... telling lies about himself. This is easy to do on the Internet. I know this happens sometimes because I've read about it in the newspaper ... but it's never happened to me.*

Do you think Internet relationships can ever be as strong as traditional relationships?

***I think it depends on** the kind of relationship. Before the Internet, people used to have pen friends. They wrote letters to each other and sometimes those pen friends became very close and that can also happen on the Internet.*

Are relationships formed in childhood different from those formed in adolescence and adulthood?

***Yes, I think so.** Children like to play with their friends, but adolescents just like to hang out with their friends and talk a lot. I guess adults make friends at work.*

Thank you.]

26. Pair work—practice

Unit 6 Advertising

1-2. Pair work—many possible answers

3. Audio and answers

a. [*Audio: It's an ad for pink insulation wool—you know, for putting inside the walls of houses to keep them warm... it's been on TV quite a lot lately. You can see it every night at least 2 or 3 times.*]
television

b. [*Audio: Well, I saw a really funny ad for chocolate chip cookies the other day. It was on someone's t-shirt... it had a humorous cartoon picture on the front, with a girl running away from a raisin cookie, and on the back, she was smiling and eating a really delicious chocolate chip cookie.*]
clothing

c. [*Audio: There's an advert for the local zoo that I keep hearing on the radio. It's got this really annoying jingle, so it sticks in your head... and I just can't stand it!*]
radio

d. [*Audio: I saw a really great ad last week. It was on a poster that'd been put up on lamp posts and shop fronts around*

town. It was for a Canadian circus that was coming to town, and I remember it because it had an amazing photo of one of the acrobats hanging upside down on a swing, high in the air.]
poster

e. [*Audio: There's been an advert in the paper recently, calling for organ donors. The reason it stands out from the other pages is that it's mostly white, except for bold black writing in the middle, and a small black and white photo showing a sick child in hospital waiting for a transplant.*]
newspaper

4. Individual work

5. Pair work

6. a. Strong [*Audio: Yes, I **can** see it.*] (*emphasize the word "can"*)
b. Weak [*Audio: You can see it on **TV**.*]

7. a. [*Audio: can; apple; advertising; can*]
b. [*Audio: you can see; in China; in the media; you can see*]

8. a. [*Audio: Yes, I **can** see it.*]
b. [*Audio: You can see it on **TV**.*]

9. a. Unstressed [*Audio: I can't understand why not.*]
b. Stressed [*Audio: You **can't** see it on TV.*]

10. [*Audio: can't; dance; chance; can't*]

11. a. [*Audio: I can't understand why not.*]
b. [*Audio: You can't see it on TV.*]

12.

Contraction	Long form
can't	cannot
isn't	is not
don't	do not
didn't	did not
she's	she is

13. Listen and repeat
[*Audio:*
can't—cannot; *isn't—is not;*
don't—do not; *didn't—did not;*
she's—she is]

14.

Contraction	Long form
doesn't	*does not*
won't	*will not*
they're	*they are*
it's	*it is*
aren't	*are not*

15. Listen and repeat
[*Audio:*
does not—doesn't; *will not—won't;*
they are—they're; *it is—it's;*
are not—aren't]

16. a. [*Audio: You can't see the people because it's a radio ad.*]
b. [*Audio : In the picture, he's wearing a funny costume.*]
c. [*Audio: There's been an interesting ad in the paper recently.*]
d. [*Audio: There isn't any colour; it's completely black and white.*]
e. [*Audio: There's a group of people in colourful clothes, and they're all laughing.*]

17. a. cannot b. he is
c. there has d. is not ; it is
e. there is ; they are

18. Individual work

19. [*Audio: A great ad I've seen recently is the one for Super-Soft toilet paper. I know it's not a very exciting product, but the ad really caught my attention and I suppose toilet paper's fairly useful—it's just not something you think about an awful lot.*
Anyway, I've seen it quite a few times lately—you can see it on television at least 2 or 3 times most nights. I don't usually pay much attention to the ads on TV. In fact, I generally turn the sound down when they're on, because I can't stand them—they're so loud and annoying!
But this one's different because there's no talking, and no loud actors shouting at you to "buy now". The main character's a very cute, fluffy dog called Softy—he looks all white and soft like the toilet paper—and he's running around inside a huge house unravelling rolls and rolls of toilet paper. In the end, the whole house is filled with toilet paper, and the dog's all wrapped up in toilet paper. It's very funny!
I remember it mostly because of the music. When you look at it—the elegant house, the expensive breed of dog, and the colour white everywhere—you expect to hear elegant music too, like maybe classical or opera. But instead, they play this really fast rock music, and the dog runs around in time to the music. It's very amusing—especially when you see it for the first time.]
a. toilet paper b. television
c. humorous d. the rock music

20. Individual work

21. Individual work

22. Pair work

23. a. bad [*Audio: Well, I don't think it's very ethical.*]
b. bad [*Audio : In my opinion, these kinds of ads are largely responsible for the low self-esteem of many young girls and women.*]
c. okay [*Audio: I don't believe it's always possible to show the true price, especially for air fares. Often the taxes are changed by the government, and the advertisers can't control that.*]
d. okay [*Audio: Well, it's really the advertiser's job to make the product look good, so I don't feel it's that bad.*]

24. Replay previous audio files
a. don't think b. my opinion
c. don't believe d. don't feel

25. Pairwork—practice using examples given

26-28. Individual/Pair work—practice

Unit 7 Further Study and Future Plans

1. [*Audio*
i. Right, let's talk about what you do. Do you work or are you a student?
ii. What subjects are you studying?
iii. Is biology a difficult subject?

iv. What's the most interesting aspect of biology?
v. What's the least interesting aspect of biology?]

2. Answer a = question ii above
Answer b = question iii above
Answer c = question v above
Answer d = question i above
Answer e = question iv above

3-4. Pair work—practice

5. Pair work—prediction

a. MBA b. dream c. English
d. Australia/NZ e. reputable f. get ahead
g. expensive h. run a business

[*Audio*
A course I would love to take in the future is a Master of Business Administration, an MBA. This has been my dream for so long, and part of my goal is to study an MBA in an English speaking country, such as Australia or New Zealand, because here in China a degree from a reputable foreign university really helps you to get ahead. Anyway, the course involves studying lots of different subjects, including marketing, accounting, finance and project management. It involves studying theory as well as practical examples, which I think is really useful. It takes about two years full time, and studying overseas is very expensive, but it's worth it to get an international education. I'd prefer to study in Australia or New Zealand, as I've heard the environment and climate in both countries are very good and they are quite safe places to live. Of course, before I study my Masters I need to finish my undergraduate degree here at the Nanjing University. The reason I want to study an MBA is because in the future, I hope to run my own import/export business and be a successful business owner.]

6. [*Audio*
Examiner: After you completed your MBA studies, do you think you would want to do further study?
Candidate: Ah, no...I think that would be enough. I will need to make some money after that!
Examiner. Yes. And, do you normally find it easy or difficult to learn new things?
Candidate: Um, it depends. I think it depends on whether I am interested in what I am learning or not. How motivated I am, you know...
Examiner: Thank you.]

7. Individual work—dictionary work

8. Stress

goal — get ahead — reputable
successful — undergraduate degree — master's degree
university — to run — motivated

9. [*Audio*
goal — *get* ***ahead*** — ***reput****able*
*suc****cess****ful* — ***un****dergraduate degree* — ***mas****ter' degree*
*uni****ver****sity* — *to* ***run*** — ***mot****ivated*

10. a. Candy is extremely motivated to pass her IELTS test with band 7, because she wants to study art in London. She works very hard on her English.
b. Oxford University in England is very reputable. It has a long history of excellent education and is well known all over the world.
c. Joe's main goal this year is to get good marks on his end of year exams.
d. My professor thinks the top university in China is Tsinghua, because students who study there have an excellent pass rate.
e. Diana wants to pass her Master's degree so she can be promoted and run the advertising department at her job.
f. Finn is studying his undergraduate degree at South China Agricultural University, but he hopes to study his Master's degree at Auckland University in New Zealand.
g. She has been quite successful at studying languages—she speaks English, Mandarin, Korean and Greek!
h. Grant knew he had to get ahead of the other students in his class, so he started taking extra English classes in order to be better than his classmates.

11. Read sentence

12. [*Audio*

I'm a student at high school.

I'maSTUdentatHIGHschool — *ooOooOo* *DedeDAdedeDAde*]

13. Students say sentences

14. Answers and [*Audio*

PHRASE	***STRESS***
I'm studying biology, English, maths, physics and chemistry.	*OooooOoo, Oo, O,OooOoo* *DAdadadadaDAdada,Dada,DA,* *DAdadaDAdada*
I don't find it difficult, because I enjoy studying science.	*oOooOoo,ooooOoooOo* *daDAdadaDAdada,* *dadadadaDAdadadaDAda*
I have a good teacher.	*oooOOo* *dadadaDADAda*
The most interesting aspect?	*ooOoooo (In speech, we usually drop one syllable in the word 'interesting')* *dadaDAdadadada*
I think it's how biology applies to people and everyday life.	*oooooOooooOooooO* *dadadadadaDAdadadadadaDAdada* *dadadaDA*]

15. Listen and repeat

16. Individual work

17. Individual work (use sentence starters provided)

18. Pair work—practice

19. a. surfing
b. difficult (people say it is really difficult)
[*Audio*
I'd really like to learn to surf. Whenever I see people out on the water, they look like they are having so much fun! So there is a course that I've found, which you can just do for a day down on the coast. They give you all the gear that you need, you know, like a wetsuit and a surfboard and so on, and they run classes the

whole day. They actually teach you on the beach and in the water. I think they teach you how to balance on the surfboard, ... uhhmm ... how to paddle, how to keep safe and how to stand up on the board, of course! Then after that you can choose to sign up for a longer course, which runs every Saturday. I've talked to some people who've done it, and they say the tutors are friendly and professional. It's one of my dreams to be able to surf because I love the sea, and I love swimming, so surfing feels like the next step. And it looks so exciting, plus it's such a good way to keep fit. And all the cute boys go surfing! But people say it's really difficult and takes a lot of time, effort and practice, so I might have to wait until I've finished my exams this year, and take up surfing in the summer.]

20. gear (n): equipment you need to be able to do an activity
take up (v): start, begin to do

21-22. Individual and pair work

23. [*Audio*
Examiner: *Could you tell me how you think the high school curriculum has changed in your country since the last century?*
Candidate: *Oh, mmm, curriculum. Do you mean what we do at school? The different subjects we study?*
Examiner: *Yes. Subjects or courses of study.*
Candidate: *Well, actually I believe the school curriculum at high school has changed considerably. Students nowadays take subjects which didn't even exist at the beginning of last century, such as computer science.*]

25. Meaning of words:
Methods: A way of doing something
Status: How important something is to other people
Gap year: A year when you don't study. Maybe you get a job or travel instead.

28. Meaning of words:
Education system: Everything about education ... the schools, the teachers, the age that children begin different schools, the subjects students study, homework, exams etc
Alter: Change
Characteristics: Qualities and skills, personality.

Unit 8 The Natural Environment

1. Individual work—many possible answers

2-3. ***Nouns***

traffic	beaches	mountain	stores
highways	seasons	trees	weather
lake	park	path	picnic
population	pollution	environment	industry
fall			

Adjectives

suburban	crowded—negative
historic	overcrowded—negative
polluted—negative	sprawling—negative
grey and gloomy—negative	
clean	
beautiful	

4. Answers and [*Audio*

traffic	*weather*	*environment*	*polluted*
beaches	*lake*	*industry*	*sprawling*
mountains	*park*	*fall*	*grey and*
stores	*path*	*suburban*	*gloomy*
highways	*picnic*	*crowded*	*clean*]
seasons	*population*	*historic*	
trees	*pollution*	*overcrowded*	

5. Answers and [*Audio:*

light, light	*praying, praying*	*wrap, wrap*
lake, lake	*rot, rot*	*lace, lace*
rice, rice	*lay, lay*	*ramp, ramp*
low, low	*lane, lane*	*leap, leap*
wrong, wrong	*lamb, lamb*	*lock, lock*]

6. Individual / Pair work—practice

7. Answers and Audio
a. Speaker 2 d. Speaker 4
b. Speaker 5 e. Speaker 3
c. Speaker 1
[*Audio*
Speaker 1
Our town is a beautiful historic city, and a very international place but not overcrowded. There are lots of trees and nice people. The weather is very grey and gloomy in winter, but it's nice to live in beautiful Amsterdam, Netherlands
Speaker 2
I live in an apartment in a big city. It's crowded, lots of traffic at all times of the day causing pollution. It's too hot most of the time. We have some beautiful beaches here in central Florida but I never get to them any more. I'd love to move. I'd go to the mountains any day.
Speaker 3
We have mountains and a beach nearby. The mountains are 15 minutes drive away and the beach is 20 minutes drive away. So people often drive to the mountains and spend the day walking, or go to the beach and enjoy swimming, although the beaches can become very crowded in the summer.
Speaker 4
In the heart of the city is a lake surrounded by a park with a cycling and walking track. The lake is clean and beautiful. Families often take picnics there and you can see people swimming, playing frisbee, rollerblading, all kinds of activities.
Specker 5
Well, it's a sprawling suburban area with few stores or highways. There's not much industry and the environment is not polluted. We get year round seasons, particularly a gorgeous fall. Unfortunately, the people keep to themselves most of the time and it's hard to make friends.]

8. *a. Where do you live? In an apartment or a house?*
b. What is the area like where you live?
c. Describe the town or city where you live?
d. Where do people go at the weekend to enjoy some fresh air?
e. How do people enjoy the outdoors where you live?

9. Pair work—role play

10. Answers and [*Audio*
Hi, I'm Maddi
Try to cut down on your carbon footprint for the environment.

Travel by bike or on foot instead of using the car whenever possible. Turn lights off the when you leave the room. Take shorter and cooler showers. Conserve water. Recycle for sure!

My name's Chloe

We ought to recycle some goods. People think that recycling is so good for the environment, but the truth is, it really isn't that great. You have to use fossil fuels for the energy to break it down and then make a new product out of it. We should try to reuse things instead.

I'm Rachel

There are lots of ways to help the environment and earth. A big one is to stop junk mail. In the US junk mail is equal to 100 million trees per day.

Hi, I'm Stacy

I've always thought we should go back to the basics. If everyone would quit throwing trash on the ground it would be a huge step in the right direction. Sounds simple, but drive down a highway and look to your left and right and you'll see what I mean.

My name's Michael

Sell your car, your house, and most belongings. Live in a brush hut, eat berries, wear leaves for clothes, and move every 2 months.

I'm Jane

Well you could drive a car with bio-diesel but that's not going to make a difference when massive companies keep pumping out the goods.]

a. Maddi b. Maddi
c. Chloe d. Stacy
e. Michael

11-12. Examples for students

13. [*Audio*

a. You should try to cut down your carbon footprint.
b. You ought to travel by bike or on foot instead of car whenever possible.
c. We oughtn't to leave the lights on when we leave the room.
d. We shouldn't waste water.]

14. Maddi

To try to cut down on our carbon footprint for the environment, we should travel by bike or on foot instead of using the car whenever possible. We also ought to turn lights off when we leave a room, take shorter showers to conserve water and recycle for sure!

Chloe

We ought to recycle some goods. People think that recycling is so good for the environment, but the truth is, it really isn't that great. You have to use fossil fuels for the energy to break it down and then make a new product out of it. We ought to try to reuse things instead.

Stacy

I've always thought we should go back to the basics. If everyone would quit throwing trash on the ground it would be a huge step in the right direction...Sounds simple, but drive down a highway and look to your left and right and you'll see what I mean...

Michael

I think we should all sell our cars, our houses, and most belongings. Live in a brush hut, eat berries, wear leaves for clothes, and move every 2 months.

15-17. Individual work

18-19. Pair work—Practice

20. Present simple tense

21. Answers and Audio

a. A bamboo forest that is near her house.
b. One road. Many cycling and walking paths. Farm buildings and a house.
c. A large goat.
d. Enjoy nature. Walk or cycle.
e. A place to relax and forget about troubles.
f. She says she enjoys going there. The goat made her nervous and unsure.

[*Audio*

A natural environment that I like. Well, I'm very lucky to live near a bamboo forest. It's a strangely quiet place and, I guess that's why I enjoy going there. Not many people visit the forest and there are few cars as there is only one road but many smaller cycling or walking paths. I go there to keep fit and so I usually cycle from my house and through the forest. Once, I came face to face with a large goat and I was very nervous and unsure of what to do. The goat was blocking my path and I wasn't sure if I should continue or turn around. But before I knew it, the goat had run off in fright. Lucky me! I thought.

People go there to enjoy nature. They mostly walk or cycle along the forest pathways.

The forest is a very beautiful place to relax and forget about any troubles in my life. It's great for relieving stress. You can't hear any traffic, only the sound of the birds and the wind passing through the bamboo. That sound is almost haunting.

There's a small cluster of farm buildings along the path. Amongst them is a house. I have no idea who lives there but the house is very old but well maintained. I think the whole family lives there...mum, dad, kid , grandparents...everyone!

It's a very clean and unpolluted place, which is surprising considering it's so close to a city.]

22-25. Individual / Pair work

Unit 9 Cooking and Special Occasions

1. Individual work—dictionary work

2. Pairwork—many possible answers

3. Individual work—translation

4. [*Audio:*

Ingredients	*Recipe*	*Marinade*	*Bowl*
Frying pan	*Tablespoon*	*Cloves*	*Sour cream*
Thighs	*Stock*	*Lid*	*Juice*
Remove	*Chop*	*Pour*	*Fry*
Mix	*Heat*	*Add*	*Stir*
Cover	*Serve*	*Simmer*	*Marinate*]

5. Firstly; then; finally

6. Examiner: What ingredients do you need to make a chocolate cake?

Candidate: I know you need some chocolate and flour and probably a few eggs, some sugar and some butter. I don't

think you need any oil.
Chocolate: Uncountable
Flour: Uncountable
Eggs: Countable
Sugar : Uncountable
Butter: Uncountable

7. a. Apples / z /
b. Tomatoes / z /
c. Puts / s /
d. Adds / z /
e. Vegetables / z /
f. He's / z /
g. Eggs / z /
h. Cabbages / ɪz /
i. Cloves / z /
j. Heats / s /

8. [*Audio*
a. Apples / z /
b. Tomatoes / z /
c. Puts / s /
d. Adds / z /
e. Vegetables / z /
f. He's / z /
g. Eggs / z /
h. Cabbages / ɪz /
i. Cloves / z /
j. Heats / s /]

9. Individual work—practice

10. A few onions
Some apples
Many cabbages
Some rice
A lot of oil
Any flour
A lot of eggs
Any butter

11. a. We don't need any oil but we do need some sour cream.
b. There are some apples in the recipe.
c. Do you need any lemon juice?
d. There aren't any eggs in the recipe.

12. a. You have to cook a lot of rice.
b. How many chicken thighs do you need?
c. You don't need much oil.
d. How much sour cream do you have?
e. There are a lot of onions in the recipe.

13. a. Do you need a little chicken stock?
b. I need a little butter. *Correct sentence*
c. There is a little oil in the recipe.
d. There are a few apples in the cake.
e. There are a few bananas and a lot of pineapples. *Correct sentence*

14-15. Pair work—practice

16-18. Individual work

19. Candidate's Long Turn: Cooking
When I was young, my mother used to make a birthday cake every year for my birthday, whereas now I am older she always cooks my favourite meal, which is curry.
The ingredients for curry are a little oil, onions, garlic, some meat, tinned tomatoes, chilli and curry spices. My mother doesn't buy any curry powder from the supermarket, but instead she makes it herself.
First, she heats the oil in a pan and adds the chopped onions and crushed garlic cloves. Then she adds the cubed meat and fries it until it is brown. After that she puts in all her curry spices. I like curry hot so she adds a lot of chilli. Finally, she adds the tomatoes and stirs it all.
She cooks it with a lid on for about one hour and serves it with rice and vegetables.
I love curry because the taste is so delicious and spicy. It has lots of flavour.

20. [*Audio*
When I was young, my mother used to make a birthday cake every year for my birthday, whereas now I am older she always cooks my favourite meal, which is curry.
The ingredients for curry are a little oil, onions, garlic, some meat, tinned tomatoes, ... uuhhmmm... chilli and curry spices. My mother doesn't buy any curry powder from the supermarket, but instead she makes it herself.
First, she heats the oil in a pan and adds the chopped onions and crushed garlic cloves. Then she adds the cubed meat and fries it until it is brown. After that she puts in all her curry spices. I like curry hot so she adds a lot of chilli. Finally, she adds the tomatoes and stirs it all.
She cooks it with a lid on for about one hour and serves it with rice and vegetables.
I love curry because the taste is so delicious and spicy. It has lots of flavour.]

21. First, she heats the oil in a pan and adds the chopped onions and crushed garlic cloves. Then she adds the cubed meat and fries it until it is brown. After that she puts in all her curry spices. I like curry hot so she adds a lot of chilli. Finally, she adds the tomatoes and stirs it all.

22. When I was young, my mother used to make a birthday cake every year for my birthday, whereas now I am older she always cooks my favourite meal, which is curry. The ingredients for curry are a little oil, onions, garlic, some meat, tinned tomatoes, chilli and curry spices. My mother doesn't buy any curry powder from the supermarket, but instead she makes it herself.

23.

CARD A	CARD B
1. When I was young I liked sweet food...	whereas/but/but instead now I prefer savoury food.
2. My Dad used to eat too much...	whereas/but/but instead now he is dieting.
3. I like hot, spicy food...	whereas/but my sister likes sweet food.
4. We usually eat at 6 pm...	whereas/but/but instead recently we've eaten at 7 pm.
5. Rob eats a lot and stays thin...	whereas/but Rob's brother eats a lot and gets fat.
6. When I was young, I never cooked...	whereas/but now I cook once or twice a week.

24. Pair work
Knowing when to use **but, whereas** and **but instead** can be difficult. The following sentences could be written on the board to help. Also, tell students to remember that **whereas** is a subordinating conjunction.
In some sentences all three contrasting words can be used, but not in every sentence.
For example:
When I was a child I enjoyed swimming but instead now I enjoy walking. ✓

When I was a child I enjoyed swimming but now I enjoy walking. ✓
When I was a child I enjoyed swimming whereas now I enjoy walking. ✓
Rob eats a lot but he never gets fat. ✓
Rob eats a lot but instead he never gets fat. ×
Rob eats a lot whereas he never gets fat. ×
Rob eats a lot but never gets fat whereas his brother does get fat. ✓

25-26. Individual / Pair work

Unit 10 Transport

1. Answers and [*Audio*
1. *No, I don't have a car, so I walk to work everyday.*
2. *I use buses and trains everyday.*
3. *Yes, so I use a bicycle or walk to school.*
4. *I come to school on foot everyday because I live on campus.*
5. *I usually go to work by train because it's convenient, but sometimes I walk for the exercise.*
6. *My favourite way to get to school is a lift in my friend's car, then I arrive early.*
7. *I travel 30 kilometers by bus and boat everyday.*]

Speaker 1: walk / car Speaker 5: walk / train
Speaker 2: bus / train Speaker 6: car
Speaker 3: walk / bicycle Speaker 7: bus / boat
Speaker 4: walk

2.

SPEAKER 1	No, I don't have a car, so I walk to work everyday.	13
SPEAKER 2	I use buses and trains everyday.	6
SPEAKER 3	Yes, so I use a bicycle or walk to school.	10
SPEAKER 4	I come to school on foot everyday because I live on campus.	12
SPEAKER 5	I usually go to work by train because it's convenient, but sometimes I walk for the exercise.	18
SPEAKER 6	My favourite way to get to school is a lift in my friend's car, then I arrive early.	18
SPEAKER 7	I travel 30 kilometers by bus and boat everyday.	9

3. Individual work—dictionary work

4. [Audio

Public transport
Transportation
Traffic jams
Problems
Rush hour
Gasoline
Petrol
Tax
High-rise parking buildings
Cycle lanes/Bike Lane
Speed limit
Journey
Suburb
Commuters
The delay
On board
Motorway
Convenient
Uncomfortable
Break down
Increase
Decrease
Hit
Delay
Roll about/Roll Around
Cycle/Bike]
Expensive
On foot/By foot
Penalty
Comfortable
Efficient
Frustrating

5. Answers and [*Audio*
1. *No, I don't have a car, so I walk to work everyday.*
2. *I use buses and trains everyday.*
3. *Yes, so I use a bicycle or walk to school.*
4. *I come to school on foot everyday because I live on campus.*
5. *I usually go to work by train because it's convenient, but sometimes I walk for the exercise.*
6. *My favourite way to get to school is a lift in my friend's car, then I arrive early.*
7. *I travel 30 kilometers by bus and boat everyday.*]

6. Individual work—practice

7. a. What kinds of transport do you use everyday when you are in your country? Speaker 2
b. How far do you travel every day? Speaker 7
c. What transport do you use most often? Why? Speaker 5
d. How do you get to school every day? Speaker 4
e. What form of transport do you prefer? Why? Speaker 6
f. Do you live near your school? Speaker 3
g. Do you drive to school? Speaker 1

8. a. What kinds of transport do you use everyday when you are in your country?
b. How far do you travel everyday?
c. What transport do you use most often? Why?
d. How do you get to school everyday?
e. What form of transport do you prefer? Why?
f. Do you live near your school?
g. Do you drive to school?

9-10. Pair work—practice

11. Answers: a, b, e and [*Audio:*
Interviewer: *What kinds of transport do you use everyday?*
Candidate: *I go to school by bus, and sometimes get a lift in my friend's car.*
Interviewer: *How far do you travel every day?*
Candidate: *I travel about 10 kilometers, which takes 25-30 minutes.*
Interviewer: *What form of transport do you prefer?*
Candidate: *I like going by car, because it's much more comfortable, and I can chat with my friend and listen to music.*]

12-13. Pair work

14. Individual work—possible answers:
a. The parking spaces are too far from the shops, which means you often have to carry heavy bags.
b. There are not enough trains for everybody, so many people take their own cars.

c. The buses don't run on time, which makes people late for work.
d. There are traffic jams at rush hour, which always cause long waits.
e. Gasoline is too expensive so people are using more public transport.
f. Cars go too fast, which results in bad accidents.

15. Pair work

16. Prompt card B [*Audio:*
On weekdays, and sometimes on the weekend, I go to the university in the city from my house in Ranui, which is in a Western suburb. It's quite far, about 30 kilometres, and it takes an hour, but I don't mind the journey because I do all the reading for my university on the train.
Every morning I get up at 6 o'clock. I have to get up this early to get to university on time, if I go by train. So I get up at 6 o'clock and I have to leave the house by ten to seven to get the 7:15 train. It only takes about 15 minutes to walk to the train station, but I leave myself plenty of time because the trains are never on time! Often they're late, but sometimes they are early! A couple of times last year they never came and I had to wait over an hour! The trains are quite old so they often break down.
This is another reason why I need to get to the station early–in case I have to get a bus. If the train breaks down, you see, the train company is supposed to send buses for the commuters, but when this happens it takes much longer to get to the city because of the delay and because the bus stops many times along the way. So that's why I have to leave early! If there is a breakdown, I usually get to university late for my lecture, even if I leave home early. It's rather frustrating!
But I do prefer taking the train because you can read or write on board, even use a laptop! Buses, on the other hand, are very uncomfortable. They make you roll about as they move and when they stop, you have to stop writing or else you make a big mess on your paper! The last time I took a bus I gave up trying to write after ten minutes! I have been thinking about riding a bicycle to the city recently. It's a very long journey though, but it would be good for exercise! There is a bike lane along the motorway now, so it is much safer than it used to be and I wouldn't have to leave home any earlier in the morning than I do now, since cycling is quite fast.
I think I will end up cycling to university... maybe after my exams. It would be a much nicer journey I think.]

17. Answers underlined in script above

18-19. Individual work

20. Possible answers:
If they construct more high-rise parking buildings near the shopping centre, people won't have to walk so far.
If special cycle lanes are made, cyclists will be safer.
If the speed limit for cars is lowered, there won't be so many high speed crashes.

21-22. Individual / Pair work

Unit 11 News Sources

1. a. Bush will send more US soldiers to Iraq. {*Yes, news*}
b. My IELTS teacher has a terrible hairstyle. {*No. Not news*}
c. Chocolate is too sweet. {*No. Not news*}
d. Chinese astronaut walks in space. {*Yes, news*}
e. 10 reasons why you should buy a new computer this year. {*No. Not news*}
f. New Zealand signs trade deal with China. {*Yes, news*}

2. Individual work—any possible answers

3. Pair work

4. a. My parents screened all my phone calls, and censored all my emails.
b. When my Dad turned 50, he kept the news under wraps, in a veil of secrecy.
c. The city bans the consumption of alcohol in public places, and prohibits loud noise after 10pm.
d. After 9/11, there was a blackout of information from the US media—all news was suppressed.

5. Answers and [*Audio*
Do you get any news about your region from the Internet?]

6. Answers and [*Audio*
I hate computers! *Keep quiet!*
It's full of good news. *Don't waste time.*
He bought it. *It's in the news.*
One. *Turn to page nine.*
What's happening? *It's there!*
Don't forget! *Keep up!*
Tell us the news. *I agree.*
I don't agree. *It's very funny!*
Read the paper. *What do you know?*
I haven't seen it. *Not now!*
Come and look]

One.	**It's there!**	**Keep up!** **Not now!**	**Keep quiet!**
I agree.	What's **happening**? He **bought** it.	**Don't** waste **time.** **Don't** forget! **Come** and **look**!	**Read** the **paper**!
It's **in** the **news**. I **don't** agree.	**Turn** to page **nine**. **What** do you **know**? **Tell** us the **news**.	I **hate** computers! It's **very** funny! I **haven't** seen it.	It's **full** of **good news**.

7. Listen and repeat

8. Individual work—possible answers:
Yes, I have. I read one when I was in Germany.
No, unfortunately, I haven't.

9. a. How long has this been an international newspaper?
b. How many years have you bought that magazine?

10. a. An earthquake has hit New York.
b. The IELTS exam has been cancelled.
c. The latest model mobile phone has been released.

d. The Olympic Games have started!
e. Twenty-two baby alligators have been found in New York sewers.

11. a. Have you ever read an English newspaper?
b. Have you ever bought a teenager's magazine?
c. Have your parents ever stopped you watching a TV program?
d. How long have you owned a mobile phone?

12. Individual work

13. Pair work—practice

14.

REASON	Answer	RESULT
a. She's embarrassed by what happened.	F	A. My phone number is unlisted.
b. The TV program was full of violent images.	D	B. People talk about what's happening in other countries.
c. I can see familiar places.	E	C. Nobody bought it.
d. I'm worried about security.	A	D. It has an R16 censor's rating.
e. My parents were concerned about explicit content.	H	E. I like local TV.
f. There's more international news now.	B	F. Nobody talks about it.
g. The newspaper had boring stories.	C	G. It was only shown late at night.
h. This movie is for adults.	G	H. We weren't allowed to surf the Internet.

15. Answers and [*Audio:*
a. She's embarrassed by what happened so nobody talks about it.
b. The TV program was full of violent images so it has an R16 censor's rating.
c. I like local TV because I can see familiar places.
d. My phone number is unlisted because I'm worried about security.
e. My parents were concerned about explicit content so we weren't allowed to surf the Internet.
f. There's more international news now so people talk about what's happening in other countries.
g. Nobody bought the newspaper because it had boring stories.
h. The movie was only shown late at night because it is for adults.]

16. [*Audio*
My favourite source of news is the student radio station in Auckland. I get news from this station almost every day, depending on whether or not I do much driving, because the radio is in my car. It has really funny hosts, so I like it a lot. Sometimes the news items or the way they are read is so funny, it makes me really laugh. But the news items are always interesting, and informative. And I like the way they don't censor their feelings—they often laugh or give strong opinions over the radio.
The reports of events are often quite well analyzed, from many different points of view, so they are a good source of news and entertainment. I've been listening to them for years!
Another reason why I get news from this station is because they play the best music, compared with all the other stations. I used to listen to the National Radio station for news, and they also have intelligent commentaries, but not as good music! I prefer radio as a way of getting news because I don't have time to read a newspaper, and anyway, the only daily newspaper in this city is very boring—full of crime stories and sport! Sometimes, I get news from the Internet but usually by accident, as I log on to my email account. I do read the local papers, however, because they have important information about this community and at least one in particular doesn't have sensational crime stories. There are articles in it about upcoming events here and sometimes useful information that helps you get by—like sales or bargains, or a story about the area from someone who has lived here a long time. I saw my photo in this paper a few weeks ago!
I would like the paper to have less advertising, however. It makes it too hard to find the interesting parts!]

Answers (strategies) <u>Underline</u> = <u>supporting statement with reasons</u>
Bold = expressing his feelings
Italics = referring to the past
CAPITALS = EXAMPLES FROM OWN LIFE
My favourite source of news is the student radio station in Auckland. I get news from this station almost every day, depending on whether or not I do much driving, <u>because the radio is in my car. It has really funny hosts, so</u> **I like it a lot**. Sometimes the news items or the way they are read is **so funny**, it **makes me really laugh**. But the news items are always interesting, and informative. And I like the way they don't censor their feelings—they often laugh or give strong opinions over the radio.
<u>The reports of events are often quite well analyzed, from many different points of view, so</u> they are a good source of news and entertainment. *I've been listening* to them for years!
Another reason why I get news from this station is <u>because they play the best music</u>, compared with all the other stations. I *used to listen* to the National Radio station for news, and they also have intelligent commentaries, but not as good music! I prefer radio as a way of getting news <u>because I don't have time to read a newspaper</u>, and anyway, the only daily newspaper in this city is very boring—full of crime stories and sport! Sometimes, I get news from the Internet but usually by accident, as I log on to my email account. I do read the local papers, however, <u>because they have important information about this community and at least one in particular doesn't have sensational crime stories. There are articles in it about upcoming events here and sometimes useful information that helps you get by</u>—like sales or bargains, or a story

about the area from someone who has lived here a long time. I SAW MY PHOTO IN THIS PAPER A FEW WEEKS AGO!
I would like the paper to have less advertising, however. It makes it **too hard** to find the interesting parts!

17-18. Individual / Pair work

Unit 12 Leisure Activities

1. [*Audio*
a. In my free time, I always text my friends.
b. One of my hobbies is taking photos of my friends and putting them on Facebook.
c. Playing computer games is one of my favourite things to do.
d. I like to relax by reading gossip about celebrities online.
e. When I'm not studying, I like to sleep! I love taking naps.]

2. Individual work—many possible answers

3. a. playing computer games
b. looking at websites
c. listening to music
d. shopping
e. photography
f. reading a novel

4. Individual work

5. A = II B = III
C = V & VI D = I

6. [*Audio*
Examiner: *Hello, My name is Mary—what's your full name please?*
Candidate: *My full name is Ling Bo, but you can call me Charlie.*
Examiner: *Okay Charlie. Could I see your identification please?*
Candidate: *Sure. Here you are.*
Examiner: *Okay. For the first part of the test, I'd like to talk to you about free time. How much free time do you have?*
Candidate: *I am studying quite hard at the moment, so I don't have a lot of free time!*
Examiner: *What do you usually do in your free time?*
Candidate: *Apart from studying, I like to chat with my friends online for fun and I also love going to the movies to relax.*
Examiner: *Do you think people these days should have more free time?*
Candidate: *Yes, I do think that people probably should have more free time nowadays, because life is so much busier and more stressful that we need more time to relax.*]

7. Sure. Here you are.
O. Ooo
DA. DAdada

I am studying quite hard at the moment, so I don't have a lot of free time!
ooOoooOoooo, ooOooooooO
dedeDAdededeDAdededede, dedeDAdedededededeDA

Apart from studying, I like to chat with my friends online for fun.
oooOoo, ooooooOoOoO
dededeDAdede, dedededededeDAdeDAdeDA

and I also love going to the movies to relax.
ooOoooooooOoooO
dedeDAdedededededeDAdededeDA
Yes, I do think that people probably should have more free time nowadays,

ooOooooooooOooOOooo,
dedeDAdedededededededeDAdedeDADAdedede,
because life is so much busier and more stressful that we need more time to relax.

ooOoooOooooOooooOoooO
dedeDAdededeDAdedededeDAdedededeDAdededeDA

8. Listen and repeat

9-10. Individual work

11.

To + Verb	**For + Noun**
to relax	for fun
to spend time with my friends	for entertainment
to enjoy myself	for enjoyment
to have fun	for communication
to be creative	
to buy stuff	
to get good marks	
to socialise with my classmates	
to practise my English	
to meet new people	
to communicate with my friends	
to keep in touch with friends overseas	

12. [*Audio*
I like to chat with my friends online for fun.
I also love going to the movies to relax.]

13. [*Audio*
a. I like to take photos for fun.
b. I use Facebook to keep in touch with my friends.
c. I read novels in my spare time for relaxation.
d. I study English in my free time to get good marks.
e. I play computer games to have fun.]

14-16. Individual / Pair work

17. Prediction (favourite leisure activity = chatting online)

18. THIRD SECTION: You are never alone on sites like Facebook and Xiaonei, because of the way they work. So I guess this is a type of leisure activity which I'm always doing with friends, whether I am actually with them or not! It is so popular with me and my friends, and I think it will just get more popular in the future.
FIRST SECTION: *Well, I guess one of my favourite leisure activities is posting on Xiaonei, which is a Chinese website. Actually, it's really similar to Facebook, but it was started by a couple of Chinese university students. You can invite people to be your 'friends' and then you can chat with them, and share all sorts of stuff: photos, music, videos, gossip, join groups … anything really!*
FOURTH SECTION: I like Xiaonei because I can keep up

with what all my friends are up to, and it doesn't matter if they are in Shanghai or Sydney, so it's a really good way to keep in touch. The other reason I like it is that you don't have to send a long email to keep in touch, you can just send someone a smiley face or whatever to let them know you are thinking about them. And the photo feature is great, I mean you get to see all these photos of your friends and you don't have to wait ages for them to download as an attachment. And you can set up your own page to be quite personal, which I like, because you can be a bit creative.

SECOND SECTION: And you can use it anywhere, well anywhere where you have the Internet. So I use it at home on my laptop, or at an Internet café, and yeah, I probably use it almost every day, I would say. I'm getting addicted to it!

19.

up to	doing
keep in touch	stay in contact with someone
set up	create/start
to wait ages	to wait for a long time
whatever	any or everything
popular	lots of people like it
stuff	things

20. Pair work

21-25. Individual / Pair work

Unit 13 Technology and Equipment

1. Pair work—many possible answers

2. Pair work—Some possible answers:

housework:	automatic vacuum cleaners, remote control dish washers
entertainment:	home movie screens, huge shows using technology
studying:	study at home, international teachers online
shopping:	shop online, everybody grow own vegetables
communication:	video telephones, 3 dimensional images
work:	work from home, flexible hours
transport:	flying cars, more bicycles
diet:	more aware of dietary needs, grow own food more

3. Speaker 1: Transport
Speaker 2: Studying
Speaker 3: Entertainment/Communication/Shopping
Speaker 4: Entertainment
Speaker 5: Diet
[*Audio*
Speaker 1: *I think people could definitely fly around in little cars which'll be like personal mini-aeroplanes. It'll be so much faster and better than sitting in traffic!*
Speaker 2: *Well, I'm sure I won't have to go to school anymore! Everything will be done over the Internet in virtual classrooms. And hopefully it'll be so much easier to learn a new language.*
Speaker 3: *There'll probably be lots more online computer games which players and friends all over the world can join. And if I have a friend in Sydney, I'll be able to go virtual shopping with her!*
Speaker 4: *You might be able to download movies and songs to a chip which you insert in your brain!*
Speaker 5: *We may just take a pill instead of eating real food. Not as enjoyable but perhaps it means there'll be enough food for everyone.*]

4. **Speaker 1:** I think people could definitely fly around in little cars which'll be like personal mini-aeroplanes. It'll be so much faster and better than sitting in traffic!
Speaker 2: Well, I'm sure I won't have to go to school anymore! Everything will be done over the internet in virtual classrooms. And hopefully it'll be so much easier to learn a new language.
Speaker 3: There'll probably be lots more online computer games which players and friends all over the world can join. And if I have a friend in Sydney, I'll be able to go virtual shopping with her!
Speaker 4: You might be able to download movies and songs to a chip which you insert in your brain!
Speaker 5: We may just take a pill instead of eating real food. Not as enjoyable but perhaps it means there'll be enough food for everyone.

5.

Mobile phone/cellphone	A phone you can take anywhere
Dishwasher	A machine which cleans dirty dishes
DVD player	This plays movies at home on your TV
Laptop	A portable computer
PC	A desktop computer
Playstation 3	Video game console
iPod	Like an MP3 player, but also stores photos and other stuff
MP3 player	A small, portable, music playing device
Washing machine	A machine which cleans dirty clothes
Blackberry	A handheld device, also called a smartphone, which can send and receive emails

6. Answers and [*Audio*

***mob**ile phone/cellphone*	***dish**washer*
DVD player	***lap**top*
PC	***Dig**ital **cam**era*
***Play** station 3*	*Ipod*
MP3 player	***wash**ing machine*
***black**berry*]	

7. Listen again and repeat

8-9. Individual and pair work

10. Individual work

11. [*Audio*
Well, I'm sure I won't have to go to school anymore! Everything will be done over the internet in virtual classrooms. And hopefully it'll be so much easier to learn a new language.]

12. Listen and repeat [*Audio*

I'll *We'll*

It'll *There'll*

Won't *You'll*]

13. Listen and repeat [*Audio*

a. It'll be so much easier to learn a new language.

b. There'll be enough food for everyone.

c. I'll be able to go virtual shopping with my friend in Sydney.

d. I won't have to go to school anymore.

e. You'll be able to fly around in your own personal aeroplane.]

14. Will, will probably, may, might, could, won't

15. 1 ——————————→ 5

Won't might/may could will probably will

16. Individual work

17. Individual work

18. The tense difference is: '*would like to have*' rather than '*have*.'

19. Blackberry

[*Audio*

*Okay... I would really love to own a ***** I think they are amazing, because they are so tiny, and they can do so many things! I really like the way they look— so slim and light. But the incredible thing is what they can do. A ***** is kind of three things in one—a phone, an iPod and a computer. So it is really useful, because you can do all the things you normally do with a phone, like texting and calling people, but you can also listen to your favourite music and surf the net. So I think I would use it almost all the time! I would probably listen to music mostly when I'm on the bus, or walking somewhere, like to school. And I would use it to share music with my friends. I think I could even use it to download films and music videos. You can also use them to store your photos and other stuff. Actually, you can use it to take your own photos as well. There is no keyboard, so you just touch the screen to type and send text messages. I really want to get one because all my friends have them and I think they are so useful. But I probably have to wait until my parents buy me one. I love new technology—I'm always interested in the latest things.*]

20. Answer PLUS individual work—many possible answers for 'Your notes'

	What is it?	**Why is it useful? How/When would you use it?**	**Adjectives**	**Why do you want it?**
Speaker	MP 3	Phone, iPod and computer Use all the time. Text friends, call people, listen to music, surf net Use on bus or walking. With friends. Download films & videos. Store photos. Take photos.	Amazing Tiny Slim & light Incredible Useful Favourite Interested	So useful. My friends have them. Love new techno-logy.
Your notes				

21. Okay... I would really love to own a ***** I think they are amazing, because they are so tiny, and they can do so many things! I really like the way they look —so slim and light. But the incredible thing is what they can do. A ***** is kind of three things in one—a phone, an iPod and a computer. So it is really useful, because you can do all the things you normally do with a phone, like texting and calling people, but you can also listen to your favourite music and surf the net. So I think I would use it almost all the time! I would probably listen to music mostly when I'm on the bus, or walking somewhere, like to school. And I would use it to share music with my friends. I think I could even use it to download films and music videos. You can also use them to store your photos and other stuff. Actually, you can use it to take your own photos as well. There is no keyboard, so you just touch the screen to type and send text messages. I really want to get one because all my friends have them and I think they are so useful. But I probably have to wait until my parents buy me one. I love new technology—I'm always interested in the latest things.

22. a. I b. T c. T d. I e. I f. T

23. Individual/Pair work

24. *Students can use the position of the question mark to help them.*

a. Are they popular with many of your friends?

b. How often would you use it?

c. Do you like to buy new things?

d. What other technological items are important for you?

25. Pair work

Unit 14 Money and Finance

1. [*Audio*

a. My parents give me an allowance to buy things I need.

b. I have a part-time job, so I make some money to spend on myself.

c. I saved money for a year so I could buy myself a guitar.

d. I have just opened my first bank account.

e. I'm happy to lend money to my friends if they pay me back.]

2. a. earn b. save make

c. lend d. wastes

e. borrowed f. spend

3.

Nouns	**Adjectives**	**Verbs**
wallet	mean	pay back
purse	generous	invest
bank account	poor	afford
pocket money	wealthy	loan
loan	good value	
tax	expensive	
salary	cheap	
wages	pricey	
credit card	selfish	
cash	rich	
discount		
bargain		
allowance		
ATM/cash machine		
price		

4. [*Audio*

wallet	*credit card*	*mean*	*selfish*
purse	*cash*	*generous*	*rich*
bank account	*discount*	*poor*	*pay back*
pocket money	*bargain*	*wealthy*	*invest*
loan	*allowance*	*good-value*	*afford*]
tax	*ATM/cash*	*expensive*	
salary	*machine*	*cheap*	
wages	*price*	*pricey*	

5.

1 syllable	**2 syllables**	**3 syllables**	**4 syllables**
purse	wallet	allowance	pocket money
loan	wages	bank account	
tax	discount	salary	
cash	bargain	credit card	
price	wealthy	ATM	
mean	pricey	cash machine	
poor	selfish	generous	
cheap	pay back	good value	
rich	invest	expensive	
	afford		

6. Pair work

7.

/θ/ sounds	/ð/ sounds
think	their
thanks	this
wealthy	that
something	although
MP3	
health	

[*Audio*

think	*thanks*	*their*	*this*
that	*wealthy*	*something*	*although*
MP3	*health*]		

8. Listen and repeat

9. [*Audio*

a. I think that he has a lot of money.

b. Although Thelma is wealthy, she is also relaxed.

c. I think that sink is dirty.

d. Thank you for that MP3 player!

e. This is that place where we thought lunch was delicious.

f. Health is more important than wealth.

g. He sank the boat before I could say thanks.]

10. [*Audio*

a. think *d. thick*

b. sank *e. thought*]

c. sing

11. Individual work

12. a. lunch b. magazines c. music

d. coffee e. credit for phone

[*Audio*

I spend my money on all sorts of things, but I guess the main stuff would be the things I need to buy regularly, like lunch at the school cafeteria, magazines about the latest celebrity news, and music, which I can't live without. Oh, and I also buy a coffee on the way to school most days. What else... Oh yeah, I'm always running out of credit on my mobile phone, so I buy credit for that quite often.]

13. **All sorts of things:** Many different and varied items.

Stuff: Things / Items.

I can't live without: I really need it. It's very important to me.

Running out of (credit): Having no (money) left.

14. Individual work

15. Individual work—multiple correct answers

16. [*Audio*

Candidate: *I recently bought a new CD. I buy music quite often—sometimes online, but mostly from music stores. So the CD I bought was from a music store in a local shopping mall near here, which is really good because it has lots of bargains and discounted shops. My friends and I went shopping there last weekend. This CD was good value; in fact, I got two for the price of one, so it was actually a really good deal. I bought the CD after a friend played me one of the band's songs, and I really liked it. The group is a Chinese pop group who are very famous. They sing songs about love mainly, and their music is quite romantic. I really enjoy listening to Chinese pop music, which is why I bought the CD. Local music has become very popular in China because we have so many TV competitions to find talented singers. Although I can't sing or play a musical instrument, I still love music as it helps me relax and feel good. So that's the main reason why I bought the CD: the music makes me feel great. I would like to buy more music, but my friends and I share our MP3 files, so I have a good collection!*

Examiner: *Okay, thank you. And would this item be easy to replace?*

Candidate: *Well, yes, I think so. I could just buy another CD at the mall.*

Examiner: *And how often do you buy music?*

Candidate: *Not that often...maybe once every couple of months. I download it quite a lot though.*]

17. Individual work

18. Individual work

19. [*Audio*

Examiner: *Now I'd like to move on to ask you some more general questions. Firstly, could you tell me how people express wealth and affluence in your country?*

Candidate: *Well, I think more and more people are choosing to show their status through the clothes they wear and the cars they drive. For example, wealthy people might wear expensive labels as a symbol of their status, or drive an expensive car to show they have lots of money. Some other people see their job as an expression of wealth, for example, a CEO or an accountant.*

Examiner: *And what do you see as the advantages and disadvantages of consumerism?*

Candidate: *I believe that consumerism is positive in terms of creating jobs and boosting the economy. I mean as people buy things, the need for production is increased, so more people are employed and so on. However, the disadvantage of consumerism is that people become too concerned about buying the latest product or item, and I think actually people can become a bit greedy. You know, they have to have what their friends have and so on.*

Examiner: Okay. So thinking about that, do you believe society nowadays is more materialistic than in previous generations?
Candidate: I think so, absolutely. I mean, for my grandparents, it was totally different. They had different values, and they were probably more basic values of hard work and family. Whereas today, people might say that my generation is too spoilt, or you know, materialistic. For instance, while my grandparents might have been focused on getting enough food to feed their family, some young people today are more interested in the latest movies and fashion. It's different.
Examiner: Okay, and finally, how do you think technology has affected purchasing behaviour?
Candidate: It has changed the way people buy things, totally. Take the Internet as an example. People can buy things from all over the world, so they have much more choice. For example, I can buy a book from someone in England or a computer from a company in Hong Kong. Technology has changed shopping patterns considerably and I think it is a big improvement.]

20. Pair work

Unit 15 Employment

1. Pair work— many possible answers
Others include: lawyer, judge, receptionist, doctor, electrician, builder, scientist, farmer, truck driver, bus driver, taxi driver, bank teller, public servant, postman, courier, florist, shop assistant, police officer, fireman, soldier, dressmaker, secretary, manager, dentist, musician, artist, university lecturer, school principal, salesperson, flight attendant, pilot, checkout operator, architect, journalist, veterinarian, travel agent, tour guide, chef, etc.

2. Possible answers:

Job	Duties
accountant	keep financial records; calculate and check numbers and amounts; complete tax forms; note down any errors in clients' financial records
teacher	prepare lessons; teach classes; keep order and discipline; teach after-school sport and cultural activities; write student reports; prepare the classroom for teaching
plumber	put water pipes and fittings into new houses; repair pipes and fittings in people's houses; unblock drains and blocked toilets; keep records of work and write reports
pilot	check aeroplane safety before flights; check flight path and weather; contact control tower for take-off and landing; monitor aeroplane instruments during flight; supervise other crew members
checkout operator	greet customers; scan products for price; take money and credit card payments; give change; pack groceries; check money in till
postman	sort mail; load mail into bike bags; deliver mail to people's letterboxes
dentist	examine patients' teeth and gums; treat gum disease and cavities; advise patients about dental health and care; give pain killers to patients where necessary
bus driver	greet passengers; take money and give change; clip bus tickets; drive a set route; stop at bus stops to pick up passengers

3. a. nurse
b. postman
c. lawyer
[*Audio:*
a. *Every day is different. Obviously it always involves looking after patients, but there are many different aspects to the job. I usually go round the wards in the morning, opening the curtains, and then checking to see that patients are comfortable, and I let the doctor know if there are any problems. I also do things like changing bandages and dressings, taking temperatures, and giving out medication where necessary.*
b. *My job is very active. Although I have to drive a van, I spend most of the day running around, from the van to offices and houses all over the city to deliver letters and packages. It means that I'm very fit, but I'm not sure if I could keep doing this job once I get a bit older.*
c. *My job involves a lot of reading, to keep up to date with current law. I also meet with clients to give them advice on legal matters, and I spend a lot of time collecting information and evidence about cases. My main role is representing my clients in court, where I stand in front of the judge and argue their case.*]

4-5. Individual/Pair work

6. bank teller — flight attendant
bus driver — police officer
checkout operator — postman
dressmaker — tour guide
fireman — travel agent
[*Audio*
bank teller; bus driver; checkout operator; dressmaker; fireman; flight attendant; police officer; postman; tour guide; travel agent]

7. Listen again and repeat

8. a. things she enjoys doing now
b. something he wants to do in the future
[*Audio*
a. *Face-to-face communication is very important for me. I really like interacting with people, and giving them the information and advice that they need. I like to help them find solutions to their problems.*]
b. *The news media has always interested me ever since I was a child. Once I graduate from journalism school, I'd really like to be a TV news reporter.*]

9. a. like interacting — like to help
b. I'd really — like to be

[*Audio*
a. *I really like interacting with people, and giving them the information and advice that they need. I like to help them find solutions to their problems.*]
b. *Once I graduate from journalism school, I'd really like to be a TV news reporter.*]

10. Pair work

11. i. b ii. b iii. a iv. b
[*Audio*
My ideal job would be a flight attendant, working on international flights... maybe based in Australia or New Zealand, and flying to Europe via Asia or the United States. I'd like to work for one of the major European or North American airlines. That would be my ideal job!
If I did this, my daily duties would involve, first of all, checking passengers in at the counter in the airport, preparing the inside of the aircraft for flight, making the boarding announcements, checking passports and boarding passes, welcoming passengers on board and directing them to their seats, and closing the overhead lockers before take-off. Once the plane has actually taken off, it would be a matter of ensuring passengers are comfortable, and then serving the food and drinks during the flight.
To do this job, you'd definitely need good communication skills, and you'd have to like interacting with people. You'd also need to be quite diplomatic, and good at calming people down if they get nervous or angry... Um, as far as qualifications go, the airlines generally provide the training for their flight attendants, but it'd definitely help to already have some kind of qualification in hospitality or tourism. For international travel, it'd also be important to have foreign language skills... you know, so you can talk to passengers from different countries.
The reason I'd like to do this job is that it'd be so varied. You get to work in the airport, making and changing bookings and checking people in, as well as working on the aircraft itself. I really like dealing with people, giving them information when they need it, and making sure they're comfortable. Plus, there's the international travel, and the opportunity to speak foreign languages. I like to visit other countries and learn about the culture.]

12-13. Individual / Pair work

14-15. Individual / Pair work

16. i. B ii. D iii. E iv. A v. C
[*Audio*
i. *In the future, many people will become self-employed.*
ii. *In years to come, we'll only have to work four-day weeks.*
iii. *In the next millennium, we won't have to leave home to work.*
iv. *Over the next decade, there will be hundreds of new jobs created in IT.*
v. *In 50 years from now, humans will be replaced by machines in many jobs.*]

17-18. Predictions-individual
Possible answers:
a. In years to come, the majority of people won't have two jobs.
b. In 20 years time, everyone won't have to work more hours in the day.
c. In 50 years from now, salaries will increase significantly.
d. In the next millennium, most people will sit in front of a computer screen all day.
e. Hundreds of years from now, machines won't replace humans in many jobs.
f. In 2050, people won't have to leave their houses to work.

19-20. Individual / Pair work

Unit 16 Commodities

1. Pair work—Possible answers include:
coffee beans, gold, copper, bacon, wool, rice, palm oil, nickel, petroleum (petrol), silver, coal, wheat, barley, oats, natural gas, ethanol, corn, cotton, iron ore, platinum, aluminium, rubber, etc.

2. a. wool; b. coffee beans; c. petrol
[*Audio:*
a. *It's one of the commodities that our whole country depends on. We export it raw, or use it to make a whole lot of clothing and furnishings, such as woollen jerseys, hats, scarves, rugs and carpets. Our country would certainly be different if we didn't have so many sheep!*
b. *It's one of the most important commodities that we produce on our continent. If it weren't for the coffee bean, then the favourite morning drink of many people around the world wouldn't exist. I know that I couldn't start my day without a good, strong espresso to get me going!*
c. *Well, the price of this commodity has recently increased dramatically all over the world. It's probably the energy source that most people depend on to get around and transport goods. I know that in my country, most people are reliant on their cars, but with the increased price of petrol, they've had to start walking and riding bikes to get to work.*]

3-4. Individual / Pair work—many possible answers

5. [*Audio:*

crude oil	*barley crop*
depend on	*copper mine*
diesel engine	*energy source*
get around	*grow crops*
iron ore	*rubber tree*
palm oil	*sugar cane*
price increase	*sow seeds*]

6. [*Audio:*
Crude oil is an important energy source.
Many people depend on their cars to get around.
Our main crops are rubber trees and sugar cane.]

7. [*Audio: cotton, export, gold, plant, refined, iron*]

8. [*Audio:* *cotton products* *gold mine* *iron bar* *export market* *plant barley* *refined petroleum* *wheat and barley*]

9. Listen again and repeat

10. [*Audio:* *buy apples* *supply and demand* *coffee or cocoa* *rely on*]

11. Listen again and repeat.

12. [*Audio:* *grow apples* *sow a field* *new and used* *too inefficient*]

13. Listen again and repeat.

14. [*Audio:* *car exports* *share issue* *copper alloy* *sugar and salt*]

15. Listen again and repeat.

16. know a market = /w/ four apples = /r/
you and I = /w/ we export rice = /j/
compare items = /r/ they import coffee = /j/

17. [*Audio:*
know a market *four apples*
you and I *we export rice*
compare items *they import coffee*]

18. Listen again and repeat

19. a. A commodity **that's important to me in my everyday life** is rice.
b. Many countries **which export coffee beans** are situated in Africa and South America.
c. Sugar, **which comes from sugar cane**, exists in many different forms.
d. Wheat, **which is used to make bread**, is grown in a variety of climates and soil types.

20. [*Audio:*
a. A commodity that's important to me in my everyday life is rice.
b. Many countries which export coffee beans are situated in Africa and South America.
c. Sugar, which comes from sugar cane, exists in many different forms.
d. Wheat, which is used to make bread, is grown in a variety of climates and soil types.]

21. a. Petrol, which is used to fuel the majority of motor vehicles, is becoming more and more expensive. [non-defining]
b. Gold, which is a precious metal, is extracted from goldmines or riverbeds. [non-defining]
c. Coffee beans that are imported from Africa are roasted to bring out the flavour. [defining] OR:
Coffee beans, which are imported from Africa, are roasted to bring out the flavour. [non-defining]
d. Copper, which has been used by man for 10,000 years, is mined in the United States and Chile. [non-defining]
e. The rice that we use to make this special dish is of the long-grain variety. [defining]

22. i. B ii. B iii. A iv. A
[*Audio:*
Well, a commodity that's very important to me in my everyday life—at least when I'm working—is petrol... I mean, petrol to fuel my car. At the moment it's so expensive that I think everyone's finally realizing just how much we all depend on it.
Our country doesn't have any crude oil reserves, but we do have oil refineries, so I guess we have to import the crude oil from other countries... I'm not 100% sure where it comes from, but as far as I know, the main petroleum exporting nations are located in the Middle East, South America and Africa—you know, like Iran, Iraq, Saudi Arabia, Venezuela and Nigeria. We must import it from one of those countries.
And as for me, I'm just like everyone else—I have to go to a service station to fill up with petrol. I don't pay for it though, as all of my travels are for work, so I have a special card that I use when I go, and the price is automatically charged to the company. It's not for my own private use though. I have my own car, which I use to drive around in the weekends.
Petrol is definitely important to me because I'm a sales representative for a cosmetics company, which means I have to drive all around the country to different shops and businesses in order to market our product. So, without petrol, I'd be a bit stuck. I'm not sure what I'd do, really. I can't really think of a fast, efficient mode of transport that doesn't use some type of petrol or diesel.]

23. Individual work

24-25. Individual / Pair work

26-27. i. D ii. C iii. A iv. E v. B
[*Audio:*
i. We have to provide food subsidies to people who can't afford it.
ii. It's a matter of getting around the wars, politics and corruption that prevent the distribution of staples to the general population.
iii. We need to find alternative vehicle fuels that can be cheaply produced.
iv. In the future, I think it'll be necessary for us to rely on science to help us produce faster-growing crops if we want to have enough.
v. It's important that we start looking in other places to locate more of these natural energy reserves.]

28. Pair work (can use sentences above as models)

29-30. Individual / Pair work

Unit 17 Population

1. **Physical Appearance:** Slim, overweight, athletic, muscular, bald, ugly, good looking
Personality: cruel, kind, lazy, cold-hearted, energetic, mean, lively, gentle, tolerant, practical, charming, aggressive, relaxed, anxious, enthusiastic, humble, warm

2. **Appearance:** slim, athletic, overweight, bald, muscular
Personality: cruel, lazy, warm, cold-hearted, energetic, kind, lively, gentle, enthusiastic, deceitful, anxious, mean, relaxed, aggressive, charming, humble, optimistic, intolerant, honest, generous, patient

3.

Personality	Appearance	Similar/Opposite meanings
Good Qualities: lively enthusiastic kind relaxed warm charming energetic humble optimistic gentle honest generous patient	**Positive:** slim athletic muscular	*Find words with similar meanings to:* mean—cold—hearted energetic—lively gentle—kind athletic—muscular
Bad Qualities: lazy aggressive cruel intolerant cold—hearted deceitful mean anxious	**Negative:** overweight bald	**Opposite meanings** *Find words with opposite meanings to:* overweight—slim kind—mean warm—cold—hearted deceitful—honest relaxed—anxious patient—intolerant

4. What's he like? Talking about personality
What does he look like? Talking about appearance

5. Individual / Pair work

6. Individual work

7. Introducing your choice Section D
Describing physical appearance Section C
Describing character or personality Section A
Explaining the reason for your choice Section B

[*Audio An old person you admire*

Speaker A *As I said, he doesn't smile often but actually he's a really talkative and friendly man... one of the most cheerful people I've ever met... always optimistic and enthusiastic about everything—not just history and sport—but everything. He has a great sense of humour and can always make people laugh. He's also the most relaxed person I've ever met ... almost too relaxed. He's never on time, even now that he's retired. I remember he was always late for class, late for games, late for everything. For a joke, we bought him a lovely big clock as a retirement present.*

Speaker B *He retired from teaching several years ago but he's still very interested in all kinds of sports and I still bump into him from time to time at different events. I admire him because of his patience, his kindness, his willingness to help, and his generosity. He is one of the nicest people I know.*

Speaker C *He's tall, quite well-built, and still looks very fit despite his age. He has grey hair but he's a little bit bald now. He always looks very serious, and rarely smiles. When he does smile, his eyes twinkle and his face is covered in wrinkles. His skin is quite suntanned, probably because he spends so much time outdoors. He loves wearing comfortable, casual clothes but they are always spotlessly clean and he never looks untidy.*

Speaker D *The person I've chosen to tell you about is someone I've admired for several years now. I first met him when I started high school. He was my history teacher but he was also the school sports' coordinator and I used to see him after school at soccer practice and again on Saturday mornings when we played our games.*]

8. Individual / Pair work

9.

Country	Years
Botswana	34
Russia	65
Peru	70
China	72
New Zealand	80
Japan	82

10. Pair work

11. [*Audio*

Speaker A *Hey, have you seen this chart? Guess which country has the highest life expectancy in the world?*

Speaker A *I know the answer to that question: it's Japan. 82 years is how long the average Japanese can expect to live...Why is that, do you think?*

Speaker A *I don't know for sure but their diet might have a lot to do with it. They eat lots of fish and vegetables.*

Speaker B *Oh... Do New Zealanders have a good diet too?*

Speaker A *As far as I know, they eat too much meat and cheese so it's not exactly a healthy diet... lots of protein but probably too much fat. Their quality of life would be good though. New Zealand's part of the developed world, but it's not really an industrialised country, so they've got plenty of clean, fresh air.*

Speaker B *That could be the reason for their longevity, I suppose... I thought it might be because they play a lot of sport and get lots of exercise. Look, I see life expectancy in China is pretty high.*

Speaker A *Yes, 72. I think that's the highest it's ever been... higher now than Peru where people only live to be 70 on average. I have heard that there is a lot of poverty in Peru, in both urban and rural areas. Many of the workers are paid very low wages so they may not be able to afford nutritious food or proper health care... and Russians are even worse off; they can only expect to live to 65!*

Speaker B *Too much vodka!*

Speaker A *I don't know about that... but alcoholism could be a factor. Seriously, I think they have quite a low standard of living, you know, things like the quality of housing and the amount of food available. Even so, their life expectancy is nearly double that of Botswana.*

Speaker B *I don't think I've heard of Botswana before. Where's that?*

Speaker A *Africa. People in Botswana only live on average to the age of 34!*

Speaker B *That's awful!*

Speaker A *Terrible, isn't it? I know that about two thirds of Botswana is desert, but I also know it has a great natural resource— diamonds—so it's a relatively wealthy country and it only has a small population, less than 2 million. I've also heard that it has a good system of government and there is no civil war or fighting. It even has free education and health care for all its citizens.*

Speaker B *Why do they die so young then?*

Speaker A *Disease. The AIDS epidemic. It's the worst-affected country in the world!*]

12-13. Audio and answers

Terrible, isn't it. I know that about two thirds of Botswana is desert, but I also know it has a great natural resource—diamonds—so it's a relatively wealthy country and it only has a small population, less than 2 million. I've also heard that it has a good system of government and there is no civil war or fighting. It even has free education and health care for all its citizens.

Why do they die so young then?

Disease. The AIDS epidemic. It's the worst-affected country in the world!

14. Individual work

16. Pair work—some possible answers:

a. They may be wealthy. / They could be wealthy.
b. They might be sick. / They could be sick.
c. Alcoholism may be a factor. / Alcoholism could be a factor.
d. It would be a good place to live.
e. The climate might be a factor. / The climate may be a factor.
f. The water may not be safe to drink. / The water might not be safe to drink.
g. There would be a lot of fighting.
h. They would be better off.
i. There might be a lot of disease. / There could be a lot of disease.
j. They might not have warm houses. / They may not have warm houses.

17. Some possible answers:

Why do you think life expectancy is increasing in many countries?

better diet... less physical labour
better medical technology... medicine...
better childcare... education...

There are some countries where life e xpectancy is not increasing, in fact, it is considerably shorter than in other countries. What do you think the reasons are for that?

not enough to eat... war... disease...
political corruption... lack of education...

If human lifespans continue to lengthen, in what ways will our society change?

slower pace of life... healthcare increase...
important to save own money for retirement...
more elderly people needing occupations and hobbies...

Not only is the world's population increasing, but much of the population is moving from the countryside to the city. What kinds of problems will very large cities face in the future?

infrastructure...
employment... traffic jams... housing needs...
overcrowding... crime...

18. Pair work

Unit 1B International Events

1-2. Individual / Pair work—many possible answers

3.

Individual sports (sports you can play or do on your own)	*Sports you can play or do against one other person*	*Team sports (sports you do or play in a team)*
swimming running discus weight Lifting javelin gymnastics wind surfing yachting etc.	table tennis tennis badminton fencing boxing etc.	hockey soccer rugby relay running water polo volleyball basketball etc.

4-5. Individual / Pair work

6-8. Individual / Pair work

9. Some possible paraphrases:

a. Volunteers = Unpaid workers / helpers
Foreigners = visitors from abroad
b. Arguments against = reasons against / disadvantages of
c. Infrastructure = road and rail network and all public facilities
Influx = arrival / flood
d. Traffic congestion = traffic jams / traffic slows right down
e. Inhabitants = people / residents
Inconvenienced = put out / troubled / hassled / made uncomfortable
Disruption = disorder / inconvenience
f. Outweigh = benefits are far greater (more) than

10-11. Pair work

12. [*Audio*
We flew to Beijing for the Olympic Games.]

13. [*Audio*
***We** flew to Beijing for the Olympic Games.*
*We **flew** to Beijing for the Olympic Games.*
*We flew **to** Beijing for the Olympic Games.*
*We flew to **Beijing** for the Olympic Games.*
*We flew to Beijing for the **Olympic** Games.*
*We flew to Beijing for the Olympic **Games**.*]

14. Individual work

15. Individual work—multiple correct answers

16. a. Why did they build such a big stadium?
(large number of spectators)
They built a big stadium so that they can hold a large number of spectators.
b. Why did they hold a press conference?
(update the media)
They held a press conference to update the media./so that they could update the media.

c. Why was there traffic restriction?
(reduce air pollution)
There was traffic restriction to reduce air pollution./so that they could reduce air pollution.

d. Why did they use remote video monitoring?
(check food hygiene)
They used remote video monitoring to check food hygiene./so that they could check food hygiene.

e. Why did they build special ramps?
(wheelchairs)
They built special ramps for wheelchairs.

17. Answers and [*Audio*
I think there are a number of reasons for this. As far as I can see, the main purpose is to impress other countries, ... to raise their status in the world ... and maybe to improve international relations I also believe governments like to host big events so that they can attract overseas visitors who will spend a lot of money ... Yes, they do it for profit, as well, I think.]

Reasons why governments host international events:

To impress other countries
To raise their status in the world
To improve international relations
To attract overseas visitors
So that overseas visitors will spend a lot of money
For profit

[*Audio*
Spending on infrastructure will be necessary to upgrade public facilities. They will need to build more hotels, of course, for accommodation. They will also need a good public transportation system so that visitors can get around the city easily.]

Why the need to spend more on infrastructure:

To upgrade public facilities
To build more hotels for accommodation
For a good public transport system
So that visitors can get around easily

18. Individual / Pair work

19. [*Audio*
What are some of the possible drawbacks faced by the country hosting the event?]
[*Audio*
What are the main problems affecting international sport today, in your opinion?]
[*Audio*
Do you think international sport competitions are more likely to divide countries or bring them closer together?]

Unit 19 Communication

1. Pair work—many possible answers

2.

A	B
a. keyboarding	iii. typing
b. memory	viii. information storage facility
c. display	iv. show on the screen
d. user-friendly	ix. well-designed and easy to use
e. laptop	vi. small portable computer
f. scroll	vii. move up or down
g. data	i. information
h. store	v. save
i. cutting-edge	ii. ultra-modern

3. Possible answers:

b. A word-processor enables you to type documents.
c. A flash-drive allows you to store information.
d. A wireless connection enables you to connect to the Internet without a modem.
e. Email allows you to send and receive messages.
f. A printer enables you to print a document.
g. A browser allows you to surf the web.
h. A search engine allows you to search for information on the Internet and access a website.
i. An instant messenger enables you to chat with friends.
j. A microphone enables you to record sound and chat with friends.
k. Speakers allow you to listen to music and chat to friends.
l. A digital camera enables you to take photos.

4. Individual / Pair work

5. Individual work

6-7. Individual / group work

8. a. Would you recommend this site to a friend?
Yes, I would./ No, I wouldn't.
b. Do you enjoy surfing the net?
Yes, I do. / No, I don't.
c. Was it hard to find this site?
Yes, it was. / No, it wasn't.
d. Will you tell other people about this site?
Yes, I will. / No, I won't.
e. Did you learn much from it?
Yes, I did. / No, I didn't.
f. Is it suitable for very young people?
Yes, it is. / No, it isn't.

9-10. Group work

11-12. Answer and [*Audio:*
...whether they should do something else.// They could check prices for their produce / so they would know / whether the buyer was offering them a fair price.// Another thing that would be really useful / would be all kinds of information / such as medical advice / and farming advice of course / but I suppose the most important thing / would be access to education.// You know children / and not just children / in remote villages / could have school lessons.// Also / if poor people in the countryside / needed to move to town / to find work / they would be able to check on jobs in the nearest town.//]

13. [*Audio*
Speaker A: *Well, you've talked about a particular website and now I'd like to ask you a few more general questions. Let's begin by talking about communication technology. Can you tell me how modern communication technology has changed people's lives?*
Speaker B: *Well, I think in many ways it has made our lives easier. Everything is so convenient... and communication nowadays is so ins... instant..., you know, it happens immediately. We can contact our friends and family, do our business and...*

banking at any time of the day or night ... in any part of the world.

Speaker A: *Yes, it's instantaneous, but do you think communication technology has had any negative impact on the quality of people's lives?*

Speaker B: *Negative impact, mmm, well, actually it has probably had a negative impact on our privacy. There are always interruptions in our lives. Someone is always texting or the phone is ringing. You can't get away from it. And mobile phones these days can take your picture and you don't know that someone has got your picture. There's a lot of Internet addiction too. Young people especially, play on the computer for hours and hours and they forget how to socialise.*

Speaker A: *Some people say our lives are dominated by computers. Do you agree?*

Speaker B: *Oh, definitely. Computers are everywhere in our lives—at home, at work, in factories, in the shops—nearly everything has a microchip in it these days. Yes, to some extent, computers control our lives.*

Speaker A: *So, would you say society is safer because of communication technology?*

Speaker B: *Yes and no. In lots of ways, society is safer. If I am lost or in trouble, I can get help immediately if I have my mobile phone with me. But, some people, well, they don't use technology in a good way.*

Speaker A: *What do you mean?*

Speaker B: *There are some people who use the Internet for really bad things, like... hacking...and criminals. Criminals use technology too. I guess, in some ways, technology makes crime easier. On the other hand, police can use technology to catch them, too.*

Speaker A: *Do you think older people have a different attitude towards new technology?*

Speaker B: *Mmm. Yes. Older people don't usually like new technology. They think it is difficult to use.*

Speaker A: *Let's talk about technology in the developing world. How can communication technology, such as the Internet, help people in developing countries?*

Speaker B: *That's a good question. If it is in their language, it will help them a lot. It can give them new ideas, they can learn new skills and get a lot of good information.*

Speaker A: *If poor people in developing countries had access to the Internet in their language, what kinds of information would be most helpful or of most interest to them?*

Speaker B: *Firstly, I think they would find weather forecasts most helpful. If they checked the weather forecast, they could find out the best time to go fishing, or plant their crops, or harvest them. Secondly, if they needed to leave their village to find work, they could check job websites to find out the nearest town with available work. Actually, there are many things that could help them... They could get farming advice, medical advice... and... education. Education is probably the most helpful and the most important.*]

14-15. Individual work—some possible answers:

a. If they checked weather forecasts, they could find out the best time to go fishing / plant their crops / harvest their crops.

b. If they searched the job websites, they could get a job in a nearby city.

c. If they checked agricultural prices, they would know which crops to plant.

d. If they received farming advice, they could achieve better results.

e. If they got medical advice, they would experience better health standards.

f. If they had access to education information, their lives would be greatly improved.

16-17. Pair work

Unit 20 Tourism

Warm-up: A: South Pole (Antarctica)
B: Shanghai (PR China)
C: Rainforest (Amazon)
D: Ruins of beautiful buildings (The Great Wall of China)

1-3. Individual / Pair work—many possible answers

4-5. Pair work—some suggestions are:

Place	*Positive*	*Negative*
A	Growth in eco-tourism Economic benefits Money to use for research Increased awareness of global warming etc Understanding of endangered animals	Pollution Damage to environment Changes to animals' natural habitat
B	Income from tourists Increase of understanding between cultures	More over crowding Need for increased roading and public transport
C	Increased awareness of protection of rainforest Money to use for research and protection Growth in eco-tourism	Damage to forest Pollution Disturbance to local inhabitants
D	Income from tourists Appreciation of history and culture	Damage to site Too many visitors

6-7. Individual / Pair work—some possible sentences:

The economic benefits outweigh the possible damage to the environment.

The income from tourists far outweighs the need for increased public transport.

The increased awareness of the need to protect the rainforest outweighs the possible damage to the forest.

The appreciation of the history and culture of the country far outweighs the difficulty of having too many visitors.

8. Individual—dictionary work

9. [*Audio:*

Nouns

history	*development*	*respect*	*administration*
geography	*impact*	*aim*	*regulation(s)*
climate	*environment*	*goal*	*requirement*
scenery	*culture*	*objective*	*impression*
lifestyle	*economy*	*tax*	
resources	*policy*	*tariff*	

Verbs

to regulate	*to restrict*

Adjectives

coastal	*mountainous*	*uncontrolled*	*socioeconomic*
rural	*world-wide*	*devastating*	
urban	*controlled*	*sustainable*	

Collocations

the tourism industry	*growth and development*
tourist operators	*problems associated with...*
a tourism policy	*travel by air / by plane*
tourist guide	*by rail / by train*
adventure tourism	*by road / by car / bus / bicycle*
eco-tourism	*by sea / by boat*
exchange rate	*on foot*
a manageable level of development	*environmentally friendly*
a lack of infrastructure	*ecologically friendly*
the developing world	*socially acceptable*
the developed world	*culturally acceptable*
to promote understanding	*economically viable*]

10. Individual work

11-12. Individual work

13. Present Tense to describe and list activities. Past tense to describe the journey.

14-15. Pair work

16-17. [*Audio*

*The city I've visited is **To**kyo.*

*I **went** to **To**kyo, which is the **cap**ital of **Ja**pan, with my **fam**ily **last year**.*

*My **un**cle **drove** us to the **air**port on a very **hot sum**mer's **day**.*]

18-20. Individual work

21.

Positive (agree)	Neutral	Negative (disagree or want to give alternative)
I believe in I'm in favour of	To my mind As far as I'm concerned In my opinion In my view Personally, I think	I don't believe I'm against I'm not sure I don't think Possibly, but I have my doubts about

22. [*Audio*

Examiner: *Now, let's discuss more general ideas about tourism. Let's start with tourism and the environment. Can you tell me about any negative impact that tourism can have on the natural environment?*

Candidate: *Okay, negative impact. Mmm. Firstly, if we think about how the tourists get to their destination... They have to travel by plane, boat, bus, train or car — and every kind of transport produces air pollution and noise pollution. Then, there is the problem of resources. Tourists use lots of resources like energy, food and specially water. I think visitors, especially westerners, use lots more water than the local population. The tourist facilities, you know, the infrastructure they need, like hotels and roads, results in forest being cut down or the habitat of animals being destroyed. Tourists make a lot of rubbish, also. And if they go to look at animals, the animals can be disturbed by the noise and their habitat might be damaged. Tourists often walk on plants and damage them; they sometimes take plants too, or bits of coral from under the sea, as souvenirs—and in this way they destroy the environment.*]

23. [*Audio*

So, what should tourists, or governments, or even individuals, do to minimise or solve these problems?]

24-25. Individual / Pair work

《雅思词汇词根+联想记忆法(加强版)》

(附 MP3)　　俞敏洪　编著

◎ 完整收录雅思常考词汇，大量真题例句
◎ “词根 + 联想”实用有趣，配有插图，加深记忆
◎ 按字母顺序编排，增加返记菜单，便于考生进行自测

定价：58 元　开本：16 开　页码：528 页

《雅思词汇词根+联想记忆法(乱序版)》

(附 MP3)　　俞敏洪　编著

◎ 完整收录雅思常考词汇，大量真题例句
◎ “词根 + 联想”实用有趣，配有插图，加深记忆
◎ 增加返记菜单和索引，便于查找定位

定价：58 元　开本：16 开　页码：528 页

《雅思词汇词根+联想记忆法》

(附 MP3)　　俞敏洪　编著

◎ 原汁原味的真题例句，收词全面，涵盖雅思四大题型词汇
◎ 标出听力、口语单词，有针对性进行记忆

定价：28 元　开本：32 开　页码：456 页

《雅思词汇词根+联想记忆法——写作》

(附 MP3)　　俞敏洪　编著

定价：12 元　开本：64 开　页码：200 页

《雅思词汇词根+联想记忆法——听力》

(附 MP3)　　俞敏洪　编著

定价：12 元　开本：64 开　页码：160 页

《雅思词汇词根+联想记忆法——口语》

(附 MP3)　　俞敏洪　编著

定价：12 元　开本：64 开　页码：192 页

《雅思词汇词根+联想记忆法——阅读》

(附 MP3)　　俞敏洪　编著

定价：12 元　开本：64 开　页码：232 页

◎ “词根 + 联想”实用有趣，配有插图，加深记忆
◎ 涵盖雅思阅读词汇，收词全面，分类科学

《雅思考官口语实战指导》

(附 MP3)　　**Mat Clark**　编著

◎ 分析中国考生的成绩现状，阐释评分系统的逐项要求
◎ 详尽介绍考试三部分程式，收录最新问题与话题卡片

定价：35 元　开本：16 开　页码：212 页

《雅思听力胜经》(附 MP3)

新东方教育科技集团雅思研发团队　编著

◎ 以雅思听力真题为蓝本，细分常见题型和场景
◎ 提供大量听写和分项练习，帮助考生提高听力单项技能

定价：30 元　开本：16 开　页码：170 页

《雅思口语胜经》(附 MP3)

新东方教育科技集团雅思研发团队　编著

◎ 收录口语考试最新问题和卡片话题
◎ 精选口语考试常用词汇和句型

定价：35 元　开本：16 开　页码：216 页

《雅思阅读胜经》

新东方教育科技集团雅思研发团队　编著

◎ 词汇、语法、语篇三大层次剖析雅思阅读
◎ 精选 16 篇时文，全真模拟雅思阅读考试情境

定价：30 元　开本：16 开　页码：224 页

《雅思写作胜经》

新东方教育科技集团雅思研发团队　编著

◎ 系统说明写作准备过程及步骤
◎ 提供同题各档次作文比较，方便考生自测自学

定价：25 元　开本：16 开　页码：188 页

《词以类记：IELTS 词汇》

（附 MP3）

张红岩　编著

◎ IELTS 最新词汇：覆盖听说读写

◎ 按学科和意群分类：细分至最小同义词区间，符合大脑分类记忆规律

定价：35 元　开本：32 开　页码：400 页

《雅思分级词汇 21 天进阶》

耿耿　编著

◎ 电脑统计雅思高频词汇，释义准确并配真题例句

◎ 收录雅思最核心 1228 词，方便考生高效把握词汇考点

定价：25 元　开本：32 开　页码：484 页

《雅思词汇精选》（附 MP3）

孙涛　编著

◎ 词条精选自雅思权威语料库

◎ 中英文双解释义，确保词义注释的准确性

定价：39 元　开本：16 开　页码：482 页

《IELTS 9 分必考词汇·学术类》

（附 MP3）　李伯庆　著

定价：28 元　开本：32 开　页码：364 页

《IELTS 9 分必考词汇·培训类》

（附 MP3）　马升骅　著

定价：28 元　开本：32 开　页码：368页

◎ 用已知单词揣摩未知单词

◎ 从上下文中理解词义

◎ 借由“背诵诀窍”巧学助记

《IELTS 9 分必考短语·学术类》

（附 MP3）　李伯庆　著

定价：25 元　开本：32 开　页码：272 页

《IELTS 9 分必考短语·培训类》

（附 MP3）　林昱伶　著

定价：25 元　开本：32 开　页码：2"2页

从记忆、理解到应用，一次搞定 IELTS 应考短语！①记忆公式：不用死记，让你迅速掌握短语意义；②英语理解：英语释义，让你直接领略短语的精确含义；③例句应用：通过例句让你学会如何应用短语。

《雅思核心词汇》（附 MP3）

陆文玲　编著

◎ 根据雅思考试出现频率分为“高频单词”、“精选单词”及“挑战单词”三大类，由浅入深，循序渐进

◎ 4 项主题式单词分类，涵盖政治、经济、科技、教育与休闲等领域。核心单词配合实用例句，活学单词，即学即用

定价：32 元　开本：16 开　页码：260 页

《雅思 9 分口语》（附 MP3）

Patrick Hafenstein　编著

◎ 给出 4 大口试评分标准及 QPS 口试应考策略

◎ 提供实用笔记速记法及口语测试现场模拟

◎ 全面囊括 12 大常考主题，依照口语测试标准题型编排

定价：35 元　开本：16 开　页码：232 页

《雅思 9 分写作》

Julian Charles　编著

◎ 60 篇高分写作范文

◎ 阶段式写作学习法

◎ 高分词汇精准运用

◎ 综合练习精进写作

定价：40 元　开本：16 开　页码：324 页

《雅思 9 分听力》(附 MP3)

Justine Ball 编著

◎ 5 大题型深入分析
◎ 8 种要领彻底掌握
◎ 2 套完整模拟试题
◎ 全真听力测试原文

定价：35 元 开本：16 开 页码：216 页

《雅思 9 分阅读》

Patrick Hafenstein 编著

◎ 3 阶段进阶 逐步提高
◎ 说明式解答 题题详尽
◎ 5 大题型精辟剖析
◎ 2 套考题全真模拟

定价：35 元 开本：16 开 页码：264 页

《雅思 9 分模考》(附 MP3)

Daniel Sansoni，Patrick Hafenstein 编著

◎ 4 套完整模拟考题
◎ 8 篇高分写作范文
◎ 常用词汇完整收录
◎ 全真听力测试原文

定价：35 元 开本：16 开 页码：252 页

《雅思口语特训》(附 MP3)

孙涛 编著

◎ 收录最新口语真题和话题卡片，将常考话题进行分类、分级，实现逐级突破
◎ 随书配有 420 分钟录音光盘，内含所有话题题目及经典答案

定价：45 元 开本：16 开 页码：292 页

《雅思听力特训》(附 MP3)

彭新松 编著

◎ 洞悉雅思听力出题规律，提供最新模拟试题
◎ 针对中国雅思考生的特点和需求

定价：30 元 开本：16 开 页码：176 页

《雅思口语必备核心话题》(附 MP3)

孙涛 王冬 关新 编著

◎ 话题全面，分类合理，提供一个小型"口语语料库"
◎ 答案精准，表达地道，奉上最佳口语练习模板
◎ 选材丰富，语言生动，展示英语语言无限魅力

定价：40 元 开本：16 开 页码：260 页

《雅思考前突破与冲刺试题》(附 MP3)

Lin Lougheed 编著

◎ 四套全真模拟练习题，提供真实的考场氛围
◎ 包含详细题解、答案及听力原文，供考生自我检测

定价：48 元 开本：16 开 页码：356 页

《雅思听力》(附 MP3)

新东方教育科技集团雅思研究院 著

定价：48 元 开本：16 开 页码：192 页

《雅思口语》(附 MP3)

新东方教育科技集团雅思研究院 著

定价：48 元 开本：16 开 页码：204 页

《雅思阅读》

新东方教育科技集团雅思研究院 著

定价：45 元 开本：16 开 页码：176 页

《雅思写作》

新东方教育科技集团雅思研究院 著

定价：45 元 开本：16 开 页码：212 页

◎ 新东方团队倾力打造，雅思基础培训指定辅导教材
◎ 符合中国雅思考生学习特点，听说读写全部搞定

《强化培训：雅思口语》(附 MP3)

新东方教育科技集团雅思研究院 著

定价：35 元 开本：16 开 页码：160 页

《强化培训：雅思写作》

新东方教育科技集团雅思研究院 著

定价：32 元 开本：16 开 页码：160 页

《雅思全真模拟试题集》(附 MP3)

新东方教育科技集团雅思研究院 著

定价：45 元 开本：16 开 页码：304 页

◎ 新东方团队倾力打造，雅思强化培训指定辅导教材
◎ 重点攻破中国学生口语和写作薄弱环节，提供雅思试题全攻略